# An Introduction to the Soviet Economy

Harry Schwartz

*State University of New York
College at New Paltz
Member of the Editorial Board
The New York Times*

Charles E. Merrill Publishing Company
Columbus, Ohio
*A Bell & Howell Company*

for Stephanie

*Merrill's Economic Systems Series*
*William P. Snavely, Editor*

Library of Congress Catalog Card Number: 68-9277

Printed in the United States of America

1 2 3 4 5 6 7 8 9 10 11 12 13 14 15-76 75 74 73 72 71 70 69 68

# Editor's Foreword

The Merrill Economic Systems Series has been developed to meet three clearly recognized needs. First, it is designed to provide greater flexibility and broader coverage in formal economic systems courses. To do so, the series contains a core volume and ten books covering individual countries. The core volume presents an analytical discussion, placed in historical perspective, of the major types of systems. The individual country-study volumes, written by outstanding scholars and specialists on the country, provide illustrations of the nature and operation of various systems in practice. The ten countries included in the initial series illustrate a wide range of economic systems. Those who are involved with the systems field will find it possible to choose from this extensive selection those particular country-study volumes which fit most effectively their own individual courses. As the series is expanded to include additional countries the flexibility of choice will become even greater.

The second important need which this series is designed to meet is that for collateral reading in various social science courses. Those who teach principles of economics, introductory political science, comparative government, or general social studies courses, will find excellent possibilities for assigning individual volumes for greater in-depth study of particular areas. Each book has been prepared as an entity in itself and can therefore profitably be studied either individually or as part of a more comprehensive program.

Finally, this series will provide a stimulating introduction to different economic systems for the interested reader who is concerned about this subject of major contemporary importance.

*William P. Snavely*

# Preface

Since *An Introduction to the Soviet Economy* is this author's third book-length study of the Soviet economy, a word of explanation seems in order as to the relationship of this work to its predecessors. *Russia's Soviet Economy*, published by Prentice-Hall first in 1950 and then in a second edition in 1954, was a pioneering attempt to describe the evolution, organization, and operation of the Soviet economy as of the height of the Stalin period. It was written at a time when scholarly research on the Soviet economy inevitably had many of the characteristics of similar research done in intelligence agencies because of the stringent secrecy practiced by Stalin. At that time the Soviet regime banned the publication of all but a tiny handful of key data on production, foreign trade, wages, and other key economic areas. It is gratifying to know that that book played an influential role in helping to train a generation of Western specialists on the Soviet economy. The book is now out of date, though there are already indications it may be of lasting usefulness to students of Soviet economic history. *The Soviet Economy Since Stalin*, published by Lippincott in 1965, was a work of economic history that concentrated upon bringing up to date the story of Soviet economic evolution during the eventful years since Stalin's death, while abstaining from any detailed examination of Soviet economic institutions and their operation.

*An Introduction to the Soviet Economy* is in a sense a successor to the first book, though much smaller and—as befits an introduction—less detailed and comprehensive. It is also a companion volume to *The Soviet Economy Since Stalin*, since it emphasizes the *current* organization and operation of the Soviet economy. The leading theme in the latest book, of course, is the impact of the 1965 economic reform upon the nature and functioning of Soviet economic institutions. As compared with its predecessor, this volume has benefited much from the great reduction in Soviet secrecy since the early 1950's, from the availability of a far richer supply of published Soviet economic statistics, and from the illuminating researches of many American and other Western students of the Soviet economy these past two decades. Since for many readers this volume will be an introduction to the Soviet Union as well as to that nation's economy, the author has thought it important to include background historical, geographical, and demographic material.

Professor William P. Snavely, head of the Department of Economics of the University of Connecticut, suggested the writing of this volume. Paul Becher and Kathy Doyle of Charles E. Merrill Publishing Company were invariably kind and helpful at every point in the long process of editing and manufacturing this book. This writer's thanks are particularly due Professor Gregory Grossman of the University of California and Leon Herman of the Library of Congress who read the entire manuscript, and to George Garvy of the Federal Reserve Bank of New York who read the chapter on the Soviet financial system. Their suggestions and corrections were most helpful, though all responsibility for any remaining errors in this book belongs to the undersigned. Ruth B. Schwartz, with her usual graciousness, took much time off from her normal wifely duties and her regular job as a computer jockey to make this book more readable and to prepare the index. The author is grateful to Prentice-Hall for authorizing reproduction of the map used for endpapers. The author's employers, *The New York Times* and the State University of New York, are in no way responsible for the opinions expressed in this volume.

*Harry Schwartz*
*Scarsdale, N.Y.*
*July 1968*

# Contents

# The Soviet Economy
# in Perspective

1

The Soviet economy has been surrounded by worldwide contro-
versy virtually from the day of its birth. Through the decades,
it has repeatedly generated bright hopes among its supporters and
grim fears among its opponents. When Lenin and his comrades
conquered Russia in 1917, they dreamed of creating instant Utopia, of abolishing poverty and injustice, of lifting all humanity to
new heights of abundance. In those far-off days, more than half
a century ago, it seemed easy to those who believed in Marx and
Engels. One had only to abolish private property, get rid of the
capitalists and landlords, and give the newly freed working class
a chance to send productivity soaring. Lenin's opponents, of
course, thought him mad and deluded. They predicted he would
lead Russia into economic disaster, and they explained at length
why they were sure a socialist or Communist economy could never work.

The debate has continued this past half century and it is not
over yet. Periodically, the advantage has shifted from one side to
the other. In the early 1920's and again in the mid-1960's, changes
in Soviet economic organization caused critics to argue gleefully

1

that "Moscow is returning to capitalism and recognizing Marx's mistakes." On the other hand, at times rapid Soviet economic gains have contrasted sharply either with severe depression in the capitalist world, as in the 1930's, or with relative economic stagnation in the United States, as in the 1950's. It was the latter contrast that gave temporary credibility in the late 1950's and early 1960's to Nikita Khrushchev's boasts of swift economic victory over the United States. Then Khrushchev was purged, and Moscow admitted its concern about the slowdown of the Soviet production growth rate.

The Soviet economy has changed very substantially as the country has progressed from the peasant and agrarian nation Lenin took over in 1917 to the contemporary industrialized country that sends rockets to the moon and Venus and produces hydrogen bombs as well as virtually every other product of modern technology. During this time, moreover, important organizational and other changes in the country have considerably influenced the economy, causing it to differ greatly from one decade to the next. In a sense, there has been a series of Soviet economies over the years, each significantly different from the others. Not a single blueprint remained unaltered from its first formulation; on the contrary, Lenin, Stalin, Khrushchev and their successors changed important features of Soviet economic organization repeatedly to provide solutions to ever-new problems. Communist ideology has been interpreted and reinterpreted to justify these organizational shifts.

In this chapter we shall seek to gain perspective on Soviet economic development by tracing its course through the years. But an essential part of that perspective is a look, if only a brief one, at the pre-Bolshevik background, the nation and economy that existed in Russia before 1917. Much that has happened since that time was foreshadowed in the earlier decades. Had the world remembered the gains made before Lenin, it would have been much less surprised by Soviet economic progress in the 1930's and after World War II. After all, the same land and the same people were involved.

## Russia's Economy before 1917

The backwardness of Czarist Russia over most of its history is well known. The great liberating tides of change set in motion by the Renaissance, the Reformation, and the early industrial revolution had little impact on distant Russia. Serfdom—the virtual enslavement of the Russian peasant—continued in the Czar's domain long after it had vanished from Western Europe. It was not abolished until the early 1860's, almost simultaneously with the freeing of Negro slaves in the United States. Likewise, an autocratic monarch, a state church, and censorship of the press persisted in Russia long after they had become anachronisms farther west. And the illiteracy and ignorance of the mass of common people during most of the Romanov era hardly encouraged economic progress.

But there was a potent force for change that could not be denied by even the most reactionary Czar. It was the compulsion to modernize that was born of Russia's many wars, wars of defense against invaders like Napoleon and wars of aggression that won Muscovy vast territories. To win these wars, the Czar's army had to be equipped with weapons at least as good as those possessed by potential foes. As it became evident that better and more effective weapons were being developed in the West, the army began first to purchase them from abroad and then to produce them at home. Artillery production began in Russia before 1500. The manufacturing knowledge was supplied by foreigners hired for the purpose. The metals needed to produce cannon and other weapons required that ores be mined and then refined for their metal content. For this, too, Russia looked often to foreigners. In the early 1660's, for example, a Danish industrialist, Peter Marselis, operated the largest metallurgical and iron mills in the country. A Russian statesman who backed Marselis, A.L. Ordyn-Nashchokin, was even then sounding a theme that has been repeated over and over since: "It is not shameful to copy what is good from abroad."[1]

These early beginnings were dwarfed by the activities of Peter the Great in the eighteenth century. The story has been told often of his travels in the West, of his energetic large-scale importation of Western scientists, technicians, and skilled workers into Russia, and of the drastic means he used to set up new factories and mines. Even Peter's absolute powers as Czar were strained to overcome the opposition created by his heavy taxes, by his demand that the nobles learn the mathematics and science of

[1] A.I. Pashkov, ed., *A History of Russian Economic Thought*, trans. John M. Letiche *et al.* (Berkeley: University of California Press, 1964), pp. 214, 226.

the West, and by his ruthless assignment of thousands of peasants to work in the new mines, workshops, and factories that sprang up under his prodding. The result was a great leap forward in Russia's technical and industrial capabilities as well as in the might of Peter's armed forces on land and on the sea. Peter the Great pioneered a pattern of large-scale state-directed industrialization motivated by military requirements and based on imported technology and technicians. Much of Soviet economic history can be understood best as a greatly expanded version of the economic development model improvised by Peter in the early 1700's.

Serfdom—that demeaning central institution of traditional Russian society—had been born in part to meet military requirements. Its doom became inevitable, however, when Russia's defeat in the Crimean War of the mid-1850's showed that the serf-soldiers of the Czar could not defeat the free men of the British and French armies. But the operation that ended serfdom in the 1860's was not radical enough. It did not create a large class of independent peasant farmers owning and cultivating their own land, men having a vested interest in preserving the existing society. Instead it made the liberated serfs conditional owners of land that had to be paid for over a period of decades. And to assure that the debt would be paid, the village community was given great power over its members, thus curbing the more enterprising and progressive peasants. The peasants felt cheated; they were convinced they were entitled to more land than they had received, and they believed there was no moral justification for the redemption debts they were required to pay the state. These sentiments grew stronger in the late nineteenth and early twentieth century, as rural population increased rapidly. Heavy taxes forced the peasants to sell much of their grain even in times of hunger. In the stormy years from 1903 to 1906, the pressures born of attempted revolution brought changes to lighten the peasants' burdens, to create a class of individual landowners, and to try to regain the loyalty of the rural population for the Czar. These efforts, directed mainly by Prime Minister Peter A. Stolypin, proved too little and too late.

In the nineteenth century the seeds of Western learning and culture planted by Peter the Great began to give rich fruits in both the arts and the sciences. This was the century of Pushkin, Tolstoy, Dostoyevsky, Turgeniev, Tchaikovsky, Moussorgsky, Borodin, and Chekhov in the humanities. The sciences gave the world such immortal figures as Lobachevsky and Chebyshev in mathematics, Mendeleyev and Butlerov in chemistry, Pavlov and Mechnikov in psychology and physiology, and Tsiolkovsky, a pioneer in the theory of space flight. Such giants did not appear in isolation. Behind them were increasing numbers of talented, lesser figures who also made contributions. Western learning was still confined to a relatively few members of the upper class; nevertheless, this elite gave evidence that Russia had the human resources to create a modern industrial society based on science and technology.

Russia's industrial production increased, too, during the nineteenth century, but for most of this period it was outdistanced by the explosive development in Western Europe and the United States. The debacle of the Crimean War emphasized the disparity, and in the late 1850's Czar Alexander II began to try to close the gap. He put the emphasis on building railroads and invited foreign capitalists to bring their money and their know-how into Russia. Soon the Englishman John Hughes was combining Ukrainian iron ore and coal to found a modern steel industry, the Nobel brothers from Scandinavia were developing the oil riches of Baku, the German Ludwig Knoop was modernizing Russia's textile industry, and both foreign and Russian firms were expanding the small machinery industry.

But the real advance in Russian industrialization occurred in the 1890's when Serge Witte became the Czar's Minister of Finance and assumed the leadership of the drive for modernization. Witte believed that Russia needed an up-to-date industry to retain its independence and to give it the power to accomplish the Czar's political goals. The military strength of a country, he argued, "is determined not only by the perfection of its military machine but by the degree of its industrial development." And he added, "Our economic backwardness may lead to political and cultural backwardness as well."[2]

Witte's greatest single accomplishment was the Trans-Siberian Railroad which provided steel links between Moscow and Russia's Pacific domain. The project also provided a mighty stimulus for industrial development. Between 1890 and 1900 Russian production of coal, oil, iron, and steel roughly tripled and the country's rate of economic growth became the wonder and envy of much of the world. Under the spur of profitable oppor-

---

[2] Theodore H. Von Laue, *Sergei Witte and the Industrialization of Russia* (New York: Columbia University Press, 1963), pp. 2, 3.

tunities, foreign investment and technicians flooded into the country. Thousands of poor peasants deserted the countryside to take jobs in the new factories and mines. Members of this new industrial proletariat had to work long hours, live in slum squalor, and accept low pay; nevertheless, the move from the hungrier areas of the countryside represented improvement for those who made it. This economic development had to be paid for. Witte had to impose heavy taxes at home and contract large debts in France and other countries. But the economy surged ahead.

Industrial progress and gains in education and technology continued after 1900 but the pace was less spectacular than in the 1890's. Russia's defeat in the war with Japan (1904-1905) gave warning that she had not yet accomplished enough. Moreover, the revolutionary disturbances in 1905 gave sobering indications of the enormous stresses within the country. A wiser ruler than the last Czar Nicholas might have met them successfully, but even this untalented ruler remained in power until the cruel agonies of World War I. Yet the point is plain enough: Though Russia in 1917 was still backward compared with the most advanced Western nations, it was not an underdeveloped country on a par with Indonesia, Egypt, or Algeria when they received independence after World War II. The Russia Lenin took over in 1917 had well developed manufacturing and mining industries, significant numbers of first-class scientists, engineers, and technicians, numerous experienced managers, and an industrial labor force of several million persons. In addition, it had a tradition and record of economic development that needed only peace and stability to revive.

## The Bolsheviks in Power

Today, half a century later, it is hard to understand the calm with which Russia's upper and middle classes initially received the news that Lenin had seized power in Petrograd (now Leningrad) on November 7, 1917. For some days thereafter the Petrograd Stock Exchange continued operating more or less normally. There was no panic among the affluent, no extensive preparation to flee or to abandon homes and property. There was so little fear of the Bolsheviks that thousands of government employees had no hesitation about going on strike against the new rulers. For some days Lenin and his associates could not even get keys to government offices or combinations to government safes. The officers of the State Bank tried to deny the new regime money, calculating that workers and soldiers would turn against Lenin if he could not pay them. This passive resistance collapsed, of course, once the Bolsheviks started using force against the strikers and breaking into safes and vaults.

These initial reactions were born of the originally widespread belief that the Bolshevik triumph in Petrograd was an accident and would be quickly reversed. It seemed incredible that Lenin, his fellow Marxist theorists, and their ignorant followers could govern a complex state and economy. They had no experience, and the vast majority of Russia's managers, technicians, and specialists were anti-Bolshevik. Moreover, it seemed ludicrous for advocates of a "workers state" to think of ruling what was still primarily peasant Russia.

Skeptics could have pointed out that there was little in the writings of Marx and Engels to help any of their followers who seized power. Marx had been concerned primarily with attacking capitalism and agitating for its overthrow. He had been carefully vague about the nature of the post-capitalist society. It was clear that Marx looked forward to a time when men would enjoy equality, justice, and abundance for all. Marx's slogan for his Utopia—"from each according to his ability, to each according to his needs"—stirred men's imaginations, but he gave few directions on how to reach that goal.

Lenin, too, these skeptics could have pointed out, revealed an incredible naivete and innocence about the problems of running a complex society and economy. In a pamphlet, *State and Revolution*, written a few months before he took power, Lenin asserted that only a few prerequisites, such as universal literacy and a disciplined labor force, would be required for a better society. He continued:

> With such economic prerequisites it is perfectly possible, immediately, within twenty-four hours after the overthrow of the capitalists and bureaucrats, to replace them, in the control of production and distribution, in the business of control of labor and products by armed workers, by the whole people in arms . . . All citizens are here transformed into hired employees of state, which is made up of the armed workers. All citizens become employees and workers of one national state 'syndicate.' All that is required is that they should work equally, should regularly do their share of work, and should receive equal pay.

Capitalism had so simplified the whole business, Lenin assured his readers, that all that was involved was "the extraordinarily simple operations of watching, recording, and issuing receipts, within the reach of anybody who can read and write and knows the first four rules of arithmetic."

Lenin confounded the skeptics. He maintained Bolshevik power despite innumerable difficulties and emerged victorious from a ferocious civil war in which his enemies were aided by foreign troops. He proved himself a master politician who was able to depart from his own ideology when necessary. Some of his closest associates, particularly Leon Trotsky, showed themselves to be unusually able organizers. Nevertheless, Russia paid an enormous price in the years of ordeal that immediately followed 1917.

All during the fight against the Provisional Government— which ruled from the Czar's abdication in March 1917, until the following November—Lenin had promised peace to the war-weary nation, land to the peasants, and bread to the hungry city masses. The Land Decree was one of the first pronouncements of the Bolshevik regime. It wiped out landlord holdings and, in effect, gave legal sanction to the spontaneous peasant land sei-zures—the "black partition"—that dominated the Russian country-side in 1917. The decree was a most un-Marxist move since it sanctioned the spread of private property among millions of small farmers but politically it was a master stroke.

Lenin found it increasingly harder to provide bread. As early as January 1918, he urged "mass searches" of Petrograd's ware-houses to find hoarded grain and suggested that speculators found hiding grain be shot on the spot. A month later things were no better. A Western observer of Petrograd life later recalled, "The population was starving, but the rich still had money. Cabarets were crowded. On Sundays . . . there were trotting races." More and more workers reacted to the food shortage by fleeing their jobs and their city homes to return to their native villages where bread was usually available.

As the days passed and the Bolsheviks continued in power, members of the old upper classes grew uneasy, disturbed by the flood of decrees that poured from the new regime. Private owner-ship of large houses was abolished. This encouraged workers to evict the bourgeoisie from their homes and apartments so that proletarians could move in. The eight-hour work day and the forty-eight-hour work week were made compulsory by law. Elected workers' committees were given rights of supervision and control over all private enterprises, although proprietors still had the right to give orders. Not unnaturally, conflicts between workers and owners soon arose; many owners closed their factories or simply ran away. All banks were nationalized. Owners of safe deposit boxes had to open them upon order of government representatives who would confiscate any gold or silver bullion the boxes contained. Later, other decrees prohibited the payment of dividends and made the sale of stocks illegal. All of Russia's foreign debt and most of the state's domestic indebtedness were repudiated. In all of these affairs, it seemed to Lenin that he was moving slowly and cautiously, following a course that would permit him to use the talents of the managers and technicians of the old regime; to many of the bourgeoisie, however, it seemed like the end of the world.

By mid-1918 all efforts to collaborate with the remaining capitalists or to use caution in transforming the economy ended. Instead Bolshevik leaders inaugurated the period that has become known in history as War Communism. The immediate cause of the policy shift was the growing anti-Bolshevik military threat to the Soviet regime and the concurrent decline in industrial production. To many of Lenin's followers, War Communism appeared to be the realization of Marx's blueprint. Their attitude of innocent, Utopian optimism was similar to that of Mao Tse-tung when he formed the Peoples Communes and launched China on its ill-fated "great leap forward" in 1958.

The system of War Communism at its peak sought to put everybody and everything in Bolshevik-controlled areas at the direct service of the Soviet state's fight for military and economic survival. A flood of decrees nationalized all factories, made all trade a state monopoly, and announced that all persons were liable to labor service. The normal processes of the market place based on the use of money were largely wiped out. Instead, there arose a complex system of barter, of equalitarian wage payment in kind, and of forced requisition that often approached legalized robbery. Money itself quickly lost almost all value in the roaring classic inflation which resulted from continual issuance of currency in a time of plummeting production.

The struggle for food became the key economic factor during the period of War Communism. The Bolsheviks needed grain to feed the Red Army and the reduced urban labor force producing essential military products in the remaining factories. The peasants had grain but they wanted to be paid for it in clothing, textiles, household utensils, and other goods. Lenin did not have the goods for payment so he turned to force and sent out armed detachments to seize food. The farmers responded by hiding their grain. Lenin's answer was to bring the class war into the countryside, to turn the poorest peasants against their richer neighbors by organizing the so-called Committees of the Poor (*Kombedy*). These were networks of rural informers who spied on their neighbors so that they could tell the armed requisitioning squads where food was hidden. This was the real proletarian revolution in the countryside, Lenin said with satisfaction in March 1919. That which the Bolsheviks had done in November 1917, when they approved the spontaneous land seizures, he dismissed as merely a bourgeois revolution.[3]

In theory, the requisitioning was directed at the rich *kulak*; in practice, the requisitioners took whatever grain they could find, ignoring fine theoretical distinctions between the "bad" *kulak* and the "good" middle peasant. A Comrade Kurayev described the situation to the eighth Communist party Congress in March 1919:

> The peasantry is dissatisfied and protests. The middle peasants hate the Communist party . . . we are destroying the peasant economy . . . If I were to bring here all the telegrams that have been received telling how the requisitioners deprive the peasant of his last horse, his last cow . . . if I could present before you this picture of real thievery, you would understand that despite all its wishes it is difficult for the peasantry to have a better attitude toward us. [4]

Nevertheless, despite all the hardships and difficulties of those terrible years, Lenin was able to squeeze enough out of the farmers to keep essential production going and to supply the Red Army until victory was achieved. But the cost was very high. Lenin was speaking the simple truth when he declared in March 1921: "In our backward country, the workers, who have made unprecedented sacrifices, and the mass of the peasants are in a state of utter exhaustion after seven years of war. This exhaustion, this condition, borders on complete loss of working capacity. What is needed now is an economic breathing spell."

The statistics told the grim tale of the production catastrophe. In 1913, Russia had manufactured over 4,000,000 tons of steel; in

[3] *Vosmoi Syezd RKP (b)* (Moscow: Gosudarstvennoye Izdatelstvo Politicheskoy Literatury, 1959), p. 345.

[4] *Ibid.*, pp. 239-41.

1921, the figure was 220,000 tons. In 1913, Russia had generated about two billion kilowatt-hours of electricity; in 1921, there was only 25 per cent as much. Worst of all, grain production in 1920 was only 60 per cent of the 1913 level, and, in 1921, grain output fell below half the 1913 level. The reality behind these figures was widespread terrible suffering and hunger, increasingly reflected in strikes among city workers and rebellions among the peasants. The anti-Bolshevik revolt of the soldiers and sailors at the famous Kronstadt fortress in March 1921 underlined the danger to Lenin's rule and the wisdom of his plea for a "breathing spell."

## The New Economic Policy

An economic miracle took place in Russia during the 1920's. The terrible wounds of 1914-1921 healed, and the foundation was laid for a period of economic growth surpassing anything ever known before. In the 1930's and 1940's, however, the price of that growth was such that men looked back to the late 1920's as a golden age of abundance. This regeneration was the result of the New Economic Policy (NEP) which Lenin introduced in 1921. In essence, the NEP junked the nightmare combination of merciless compulsion and Utopianism that was War Communism. In its place, the new policy approved and encouraged self interest as an incentive, individual initiative, the right to buy and sell as one pleased. Private trade and private industrial production were reintroduced. The farmers were told in advance that there was a maximum limit on the portion of their produce the government would take from them, and that any surplus they produced above this tax could be sold freely. The whole "Communist" apparatus of military-like assignment of labor and of payment in kind ended. Employers could hire workers as they found it advantageous, and workers could select from among potential employers. In a word, the NEP sought to restore the free markets, competition, and incentives of the old private enterprise system.

The electric effect of the new economic concessions in the summer of 1921 was described by an eyewitness, the *New York Times*' Walter Duranty:

> Three weeks ago Moscow looked exactly like one of the larger towns in France . . . a few days after liberation. There were the same air of dilapidation, the same shuttered shops, the same empty buildings, the same occasional ruins, the same subdued appearance of the people in the same makeshift

clothes. Now under the stimulus of the new decrees . . . and under the liberty of private trading, shops, restaurants, and even cafes are being opened in all directions . . .

The new stores opened in the last fortnight alone must have given employment to tens of thousands of people. The greater part of the population seems to be either selling something or working on something to sell. Every corner in the center of the city has a group of children with trays of matches, cigarettes, fruit, cakes, etc.[5]

Many Communists were outraged by the concessions to traditional capitalist ways. Was this not a betrayal of Marxism? Lenin answered that he was only retreating in order to be able to resume the advance in the future. He stressed that the state retained the "commanding heights" of the economy, as well as most of the large factories, the banking system, the railroads and telegraph, the monopoly of foreign trade. But he warned his comrades they would have to compete economically against the capitalist forces that had been let loose in Russia. Even government enterprises were put under the stern discipline of the market and the quest for profit. The umbilical cords through which the state had once nourished its factories with subsidies, credits, and free materials were cut. Enterprise directors were forced to meet the competition of private entrepreneurs and other government factories or to face inevitable bankruptcy. It is a measure of how thoroughly Stalin wiped out portions of Russia's collective memory that thirty years later many Soviet citizens thought there was real novelty in Professor Liberman's ideas about harnessing the profit mechanism to help run the socialist economy.

The "mixed economy" of the NEP, in which both private and government enterprise played key roles, produced results quickly. By 1926-1928, the ruin and hunger of 1921 were only memories, and in most areas Soviet production had regained or exceeded the record levels of 1913. The cities were full of people again; the factories were humming; inflation had been wiped out by creating a new Soviet currency. Given proper incentives, the Soviet people showed they were willing to work hard. They tilled the land industriously, restored closed factories, mines, and power stations to operation, and repaired the country's ravaged transport and communications system. But as the task of reconstruc-

---

[5] Walter Duranty, *Duranty Reports Russia* (New York: The Viking Press, Inc., 1934), pp. 88-89.

tion approached completion, a new question arose: Where should the Soviet economy go after all the resources inherited from the past had been put to work again? All concerned agreed the country should industrialize far beyond the highest level achieved in the Czarist period. But how and at what pace should industrialization be carried out? Most important, what should be the nature of this industrial development? How and where should the required capital be obtained? The many aspects of industrialization were the subject of warm debate in the mid-1920's. Final resolution of the disputes fell to leaders other than Lenin, however, since Lenin died in 1924.

Leon Trotsky and his left-wing followers urged rapid industrialization, an end to the NEP's market economy, and the introduction of full economic planning. To pay the bill, the distinguished economist E. A. Preobrazhensky urged that the Soviet state engage in "primitive socialist accumulation of capital." He reasoned by analogy. Marx had written that during the initial stages of capitalism, industrialization had been financed by "primitive accumulation of capital" through the capitalists' exploitation of the workers. Since peasants formed the great majority of the Soviet population, Preobrazhensky argued that they would have to bear the burden of exploitation in that country. He pointed out that since the Soviet state controlled all major industry and all imports, it was, in effect, a giant monopoly. It could therefore charge high prices for the goods sold to the peasants and use the resulting profits as the source of capital to build new factories, mines, and other industrial installations.[6]

Nikolai Bukharin and other right-wingers took a different position. They urged cooperation with the peasants. They saw the soundest basis for industrialization in the growth of agricultural production which would supply industry with raw materials and also create demand for industrial products. As the most efficient farmers got richer, Bukharin reasoned, they would save voluntarily in Soviet banks, and thus make their capital accumulations available for industrialization. From this point of view, correct Soviet policy would give the most capable peasants as much help as possible. In particular, Bukharin urged that all the obstacles that prevented better farmers from getting more land and hiring workers be removed. It was in this spirit that Bukharin asserted:

---

6 Alexander Erlich, *The Soviet Industrialization Debate, 1924-1928* (Cambridge: Harvard University Press, 1960), pp. 49-51.

"We have to tell the whole peasantry, all its strata: get rich, accumulate, develop your economy."[7]

## The Stalin Era

The main issues of industrialization and economic development were decided by Joseph Stalin, the Georgian who won the post-Lenin power struggle. Stalin was dictator of the Soviet Union during the quarter of a century from 1928 to his death in 1953. His forced industrialization and modernization of the Soviet Union were so successful that, at his death, the country was the second most powerful nation in the world—a serious economic, scientific, and military rival of the United States. The cost of Stalinist industrialization was enormous, however, and the tensions created during the traumatic years of his rule had still not been fully resolved in the late 1960's, a decade and a half after his death.

Ironically, Stalin seemed to side with the cautious right-wingers during much of the 1920's. He denounced the Trotskyites as "superindustrializers" whose mad schemes endangered the Soviet Union. It was typical of his early attitude that in April 1926 he publicly attacked the notion of building a hydroelectric dam on the Dnepr River, arguing that it was beyond the country's resources. But once Trotsky and the leftists had been decisively defeated, Stalin turned on his former right-wing allies. Thus, in a speech in July 1928, he derided the rightists as advocates of "calico industrialization," that is, of wanting to shift the emphasis of Soviet development from heavy industry to textiles and other goods the farmers wanted. In the next few months he destroyed the political power of the Bukharin faction and embarked on the forced industrialization of Russia in a manner that made the Trotsky-Preobrazhensky scheme seem a model of caution and of solicitous consideration for peasant interests. Soviet workers, too, paid heavily for Stalinist industrialization.

The key to Stalin's economic policy was his conviction, both before and after World War II, that war was inevitable and that therefore the Soviet Union had to concentrate its energies overwhelmingly on building the industrial bases for military power. He put the matter most bluntly in a 1931 speech to industrial executives:

---

[7] *Ibid.*, p. 16. See also Nicolas Spulber, *Soviet Strategy for Economic Growth* (Bloomington: Indiana University Press, 1964), pp. 64-66.

Do you want our socialist fatherland to be beaten and lose
its independence? If you don't want this, you must liquidate
our backwardness and develop a real Bolshevik tempo in building our socialist economy. There is no other road . . . We lag
behind the advanced countries by 50-100 years. We must make
good this distance in ten years.[8]

Stalin's economic development strategy was very simple. It
consisted of investing a large proportion of Soviet national income
year after year and concentrating that investment on the expansion of those branches of Soviet heavy industry that contributed directly or indirectly to Soviet military strength. This
meant aiming for the maximally rapid expansion not only of
Soviet production of weapons and munitions but also of machinery, steel, electricity, coal, oil, chemicals, and other products required either for arms output or for further capital investment.
All other areas of the economy—transport, communications,
housing construction, consumer goods industries, and agriculture
—were usually kept on short rations so far as capital investment
was concerned. The result was a thoroughly lopsided industrial
development in which Soviet production of arms, steel, electric
power, and the like rose very sharply while other areas of the
economy lagged far behind. When Stalin died, the Soviet Union
already had atomic bombs and was well on its way to hydrogen
bombs, intercontinental missiles, and moon rockets. But the Soviet people still lived in relative poverty; in fact, the great majority of them were ill fed, ill clothed and ill housed.

Stalin needed complete control of Soviet society and of the
Soviet economy to accomplish his objectives. He destroyed the
private industrialists and merchants who had sprung up during
the NEP because they represented uncontrolled economic forces
that could, if permitted to exist, cause trouble. Moreover, their
presence was ideologically objectionable since his goal was a fully
socialized economy. By the late 1920's, many private entrepreneurs had already been squeezed out by the increasingly strong
state sector of the economy and by discriminatory measures of
the Soviet government. Stalin simply tightened the screws on the
few who remained; he even had many of them arrested as a
means of forcing them to part with their wealth, especially jewels,
gold, or foreign currency. Stalin also acted to bring Soviet unions
completely under his thumb because he could not afford to have

---

[8] J. Stalin *Voprosy Leninizma* (Moscow: Gospolitizdat, 1952), p. 362.

unions that would defend their members' interests and perhaps even strike as workers became more and more discontented. By removing rightists such as Mikhail Tomsky from union leadership and substituting his own trusted henchmen, Stalin saw to it that the unions became his instruments for controlling the workers and inducing them to work harder, regardless of pay or working conditions.[9]

The heart of Stalin's problem, however, was the 25,000,000 peasant families who made up most of the Soviet population. They grew the grain that Stalin needed desperately to feed the cities' expanding worker population and to export in payment for the foreign machinery, foreign technical know-how, and foreign experts Stalin was importing to spur Soviet industrialization. Moreover, the existence of these millions of private farmers was a constant affront to Stalin's vision of a Socialist Russia, as well as a potential threat to his regime's survival.

Against this background, Stalin decided at the end of the 1920's to try to collectivize the peasants quickly. Collectivization would meet the ideological goal of substituting a socialized agriculture for one based on a multitude of private farmers. No less important, collectivization would permit grain to be extorted from the countryside at an artificially low price, providing huge profits when that same grain was sold at home or abroad. This was to be the mechanism of exploitation by which the peasants would involuntarily provide most of the required capital for Soviet industrialization. This was the Stalinist form of Preobrazhensky's "primitive socialist accumulation of capital."

The drive to collectivize Soviet agriculture—and to destroy the *kulaks* whom Stalin regarded as his chief foes—swept into high gear in late 1929 and early 1930. Some 25,000 trusted Communists from the cities were sent to the rural areas to lead the effort. Government officials were empowered to deport *kulaks* from their homes and confiscate their property for the benefit of newly formed collective farms. Communist party and state officials competed in a race to see which area could collectivize fastest. On July 1, 1929, there were less than 1,000,000 families enrolled in the collectives. By January 20, 1930, this had spurted to almost 4,400,000, and by March 1, 1930, the Soviet press

---

[9] Robert V. Daniels, *The Conscience of the Revolution* (Cambridge: Harvard University Press, 1960), p. 348.

claimed that 14,264,300 families—55 per cent of all Soviet peasants—were members of 110,200 collective farms.[10]

Then, on March 2, 1930, *Pravda* astonished the world by publishing Stalin's article, "Dizzy with Success." In a tone of seemingly pained surprise, Stalin charged that "some comrades" were disregarding the principle of voluntary collectivization. He gave some examples of what was going on:

> It is known, for example, that a number of the northern regions of the grain-importing belt . . . not infrequently endeavour to replace the preparatory work for the organization of collective farms by bureaucratically decreeing the collective farm movement . . . by the organization of collective farms 'on paper,' farms which in reality do not yet exist, but regarding the 'existence' of which there is a pile of braggart resolutions . . . We know that in a number of regions of Turkestan there have already been attempts to 'overtake and surpass' the advanced regions . . . by resorting to threats to apply military force, by threatening to deprive the peasants who do not yet wish to enter the collective farms of irrigation water and of manufactured goods.[11]

Despite Stalin's protestations, the truth was that force and threats of force were very widely used, rather than exceptional. Stalin had spoken out because he feared that a peasant revolt and anarchy in the countryside might prevent sowing for the 1930 harvest and thus bring on a massive economic disaster. By the middle of March, Kremlin concern was so great that a Central Committee resolution reinforced and extended Stalin's indictment of the "abuses" taking place and ordered that these "perversions of the party line" be corrected. A major retreat had been ordered, and the peasants were quick to take advantage of it. Between March 1 and May 1, 1930, a massive exodus from the newly formed collective farms took place. By the latter date only 5,778,000 members remained, a drop of more than 60 per cent in two months. But the peasants had won only a temporary victory. The pressure to collectivize soon resumed and the *kolkhoz* (collective farm) membership curve turned upward once again. By the middle of 1932, the collective farms reportedly had more peasant families than on March 1, 1930; and by

---

[10]Alexander Baykov, *The Development of the Soviet Economic System* (New York: The Macmillan Company, 1947), pp. 193-96.

[11]*Pravda*, March 2, 1930.

mid-1935 more than 70 per cent of all Soviet peasants were reported to be members of about 233,000 *kolkhozy*. Collectivization, and Stalin, had won.

Many means were employed to impose the collective farms —which the peasants correctly saw as a Communist version of serfdom—upon the peasantry. The mildest instruments were economic, ranging from lower taxes and other advantages for those who joined, to punitive discrimination against those who persisted in their refusal to join. Terror was employed, too. Time and again Communist party activists, aided by the secret police and sometimes by the armed forces, swooped down on a village, rounded up all the *kulaks* (rich peasants) for deportation to Siberia, and confiscated all their property. The peasants quickly realized that the definition of *kulak* was flexible and that anyone who opposed collectivization ran the risk of earning this label with all its terrible consequences. The peasants fought back, most often with sabotage. They burned their barns, killed their livestock, and stole what they could from the new collectives. Soviet agriculture, in the five years after January 1, 1928, lost half of its horses, cattle, and hogs, and almost two-thirds of its sheep and goats. Heavily dependent on horse power, the new collectives might have been unable to sow their fields in the early 1930's if the situation had not been saved by imported American tractors, as well as by some new Soviet tractors. Famine swept the Ukraine and some neighboring Soviet areas in those years, killing a large number of persons. The "dekulakization" of Soviet agriculture removed from the countryside several million of the ablest farmers. This, plus the large loss of agricultural capital and the continuing peasant resentment against the collectives, set the stage for the farm production difficulties that have so often plagued the Soviet Union since 1930.

By the mid-1930's the famine was over and the collective farm system was set in the basic mold that lasted until the 1950's. Stalin required above all that each collective farm deliver a large fraction of its annual produce to the state, although the farm received in return usually only a small fraction of that output's market price. To enforce the principle, the state had an important instrument in the Machine-Tractor Stations (MTS), government-owned and -operated institutions which had monopoly ownership of the tractors, grain combines, and other major farm machinery that worked the collective fields. The collectives paid a share of their crop as rent for the use of these machines.

The MTS also provided a center for political and secret police control over the farms. In Stalin's mind, the economic and political advantages of the MTS more than compensated for the inefficiency inherent in the denial of farm machinery to the collective farms and in the problems that inevitably arose from frictions between the MTS and the *kolkhozy* they served.

But even while the collectivization struggle raged in the countryside, the drive for planned industrialization continued to have top priority. It was inaugurated in 1928 with announcement of the First Five Year Plan, and was pursued with fanatical zeal until it was interrupted by the Nazi invasion of 1941. Industrial production grew slowly at first since available resources were concentrated on building new plants and other productive installations. But as these investment projects were finished and began operating, sharp output gains were registered in the mid-1930's. A slowdown occurred in the years just prior to the German attack, in part the result of the disorganization that followed the great purges, and in part a reflection of the frantic effort to convert machinery and other industrial plants to direct production of tanks, planes, and artillery.

For all the propaganda about Soviet economic planning, the reality often bore little relation to any orderly, considered, and coordinated action. Rather, the planned targets were means of inducing enthusiasm and high hopes that would reconcile the populace to the sacrifices being demanded of it. Plans were changed frequently as suited Stalin's will, and no honest, comprehensive accounting of how original plans had or had not been fulfilled was normally given the Soviet people. Failures were either ignored by the controlled press or hidden by statistical manipulation of one sort or another. As Khrushchev said in June 1963, "Stalin himself did not pay much attention to questions of planning and he was not anxious for others to pay much attention to these questions."[12] Under Stalin, Soviet economic planning was usually a cover for an all-out effort to attain certain top-priority goals—generally military production and heavy industry objectives—while the rest of the economy was forced to get along as best as it could with the crumbs remaining after the requirements of the highest priority goals had been met. The blunders that were made in such a situation added further to the already high cost of Soviet industrialization.

---

[12] *Pravda*, June 29, 1963.

Yet the Soviet Union forged ahead industrially in these years before Hitler attacked. Painfully, slowly at first and at enormous human and financial cost, great new factories and power plants were built, rich deposits of minerals were discovered, major new mines and oil wells were dug, important new railroad lines were constructed, and first-rank new industrial cities were created.

Between 1928 and 1940, the Soviet non-agricultural labor force almost tripled, rising from about 10,000,000 to about 30,000,000 persons. Most of the newcomers to the factories, mines, railroads, and stores were bewildered peasants, some lured from the land by promises of a better life, others brought to their new jobs under armed guard as punishment for being *kulaks*. Millions of this new proletariat were women forced to work because of the spiraling inflation of the early 1930's and the impossibility of supporting a family on only one breadwinner's wages. Much of this new labor force was unskilled, unaccustomed to the discipline of industry, and unfamiliar with the care and operation of machines. But in the construction camps, factories, mines, and other centers of the burgeoning new Russia, this horde of "dark people" was slowly civilized, slowly trained, and slowly disciplined.

In the late 1920's and early 1930's, the Soviet economy received a massive infusion of Western technology. Thousands of foreign engineers and skilled workers came to Stalin's realm— as in the days of Peter and of Witte—to help build new factories, create new industries, and train Soviet workers, technicians, and scientists. Some Soviet citizens were sent abroad to study in Western universities or to learn assembly-line techniques in the most modern capitalist factories. Hundreds of millions of rubles in gold were spent abroad to buy the latest machinery. Vast quantities of grain, petroleum, timber and other products were also exported to help pay the cost. Even at the height of the Ukrainian famine in the early 1930's, Stalin exported wheat, and thereby kept intact his reputation for paying his foreign debts on time.

As millions of new workers poured into the cities and towns, more and more essentials became scarce: housing, food, even soap. The usual pattern of Soviet urban life became one family living in one room. Food and other necessities were rationed in the hardest early years of the thirties, while prices soared in the free markets. By contrast, vodka was plentiful because the high profit the government made on it helped finance industrialization, while the demand for the surcease it offered seemed inexhaustible.

Soviet achievements by the end of 1940 are best indicated by statistics on the growth of heavy industry, shown in Table 1.

**Table 1.**   Soviet Production of Key Commodities
1913-1940

| Commodity | Unit | 1913 | 1921 | 1928 | 1940 |
|---|---|---|---|---|---|
| Steel | mil. metric tons | 4.2 | .2 | 4.2 | 18.3 |
| Coal | mil. metric tons | 29.1 | 9.5 | 35.5 | 165.9 |
| Oil | mil. metric tons | 9.2 | 3.8 | 11.6 | 31.1 |
| Cement | mil. metric tons | 1.8 | .1 | 1.9 | 5.7 |
| Electricity | billion kwh | 2.0 | .5 | 5.0 | 48.3 |

Source: *Narodnoye Khozyaistvo SSSR v 1960 godu, passim.*

Of course the tremendous rates of production increase shown in the last two columns are not representative of the economy as a whole. The output of agriculture, of the consumer goods industries, and of other less favored branches rose far less than that of these high priority heavy industries. For a more comprehensive view we should look at data on national income or gross national product, measures that embrace the total production of an economy. The Soviet indices for this period, however, are unsatisfactory measuring rods. It is difficult in any circumstances to measure accurately the output of an economy that is changing radically the amounts, assortment, and complexity of the goods it is producing, as was the Soviet economy. In this case, Stalin's demand for statistics that would make good propaganda compounded these difficulties. Also, Soviet statisticians are confined in a Marxist framework that emphasizes output of material goods but excludes most services—medical care, education, and the like—from measures of national income. These and other similar deficiencies make it difficult for most Western analysts to accept the Soviet claim that from 1928 to 1940 Soviet national income grew more than 500 per cent, gross industrial output rose more than 600 per cent, and gross agricultural production increased more than 50 per cent. The last claim, by the way, was scaled down to much less than 15 per cent when Soviet statisticians, in the 1950's, published revised agricultural data that acknowledged more honestly the disastrous impact of collectivization in the 1930's upon farm output during that time.[13]

---

[13] Harry Schwartz, *Russia's Soviet Economy* (Englewood Cliffs, N. J.: Prentice-Hall, 1954), pp. 126-34. *Narodnoye Khozyaistvo SSSR v 1960 godu* (Moscow: Tsentralnoye Statisticheskoye Upravleniye, 1961), pp. 169, 219, and 362. This series of volumes will hereafter be cited as *Narkhoz* with the appropriate year.

There is no dispute, however, about the fact that total Soviet production rose substantially during the 1930's. Independent calculations by Western scholars confirm the fact of significant achievement. Thus, Bergson's estimates indicate that between 1928 and 1940 Soviet gross national product, including both goods and services, almost doubled. Taking 1927-1928 as a base, Kaplan and Moorsteen find that 1940 industrial production was about 160 per cent greater. Since their index omits munitions—whose output rose rapidly—1940 Soviet industrial production was probably somewhat higher, perhaps triple the base figure. Studies by Johnson and Kahan suggest that in 1940 Soviet agricultural output may have been 20 per cent higher than in 1928, in part because of the significant additions to Soviet territory in 1939 and 1940.[14]

Even this brief survey must mention the Stalinist system of coercion. The extreme element of this system was the slave labor camps in which millions of *kulaks*, clergymen, and other real or suspected opponents of the regime were forced to work on a wide variety of jobs, from mining gold to building canals. During the 1930's, free Soviet non-agricultural workers were increasingly put under severe controls to discourage them from quitting their employment without permission and to punish those who were absent from their jobs or came late to work without an acceptable reason. Similarly, increasing pressure was put on collective farmers to force them to work on the *kolkhoz* fields and to prevent them from spending most of their time cultivating their small private garden plots.

## The Soviet Economy during World War II

Stalin had been preparing for war for many years before Hitler attacked the Soviet Union in June 1941. Yet when the blow came, it found the Red Army equipped with less and poorer quality equipment than the Germans. As the Nazi war machine rolled across the plains of European Russia in 1941 and 1942, it occupied much of the Soviet Union's richest farm area and many of the industrial centers that had been built up at such great cost since the mid-1920's. Even in the areas that escaped Nazi occupa-

---

[14] Abram Bergson, *The Real National Income of Soviet Russia Since 1928* (Cambridge: Harvard University Press, 1961), p. 152. A convenient source for the Kaplan-Moorsteen and Johnson-Kahan results is Franklyn D. Holzman, ed., *Readings on the Soviet Economy* (Chicago: Rand McNally & Co., 1962), Section IV.

tion, the outbreak of the war had disastrous economic consequences as millions of men were drafted for the armed forces.
The overall result was a catastrophic decline in production in
the areas remaining under Soviet control, as shown by the 1942
data in Table 2.

**Table 2.** Soviet Production of Key Commodities
in 1940, 1942, and 1945

| Commodity | Unit | 1940 | 1942 | 1945 |
|---|---|---|---|---|
| Grain | mil. metric tons | 95.5 | 29.7 | 47.5 |
| Steel | mil. metric tons | 18.3 | 8.1 | 12.3 |
| Coal | mil. metric tons | 165.9 | 75.5 | 149.3 |
| Oil | mil. metric tons | 31.1 | 22.0 | 19.4 |
| Electricity | billion kwh | 48.3 | 29.1 | 43.3 |
| Cotton | mil. metric tons | 2.2 | 1.3 | 1.2 |
| Potatoes | mil. metric tons | 75.9 | 23.8 | 58.3 |

Sources: Table 1 and *Istoriya Velikoi Otechestvennoi Voiny Sovetskogo Soy-uza 1941-1945*, II, 505-21 and V, *passim. Narkhoz 1965*, pp. 325 and 334.

How could the Soviet Union absorb such crippling blows, then
rally and ultimately expel the invader? In the economic sphere,
the core of the answer lies in the virtually complete mobilization
of the country's remaining resources for the needs of the war. Every factory that could be converted to the production of arms or
other military necessity was converted. The production of non-
essential civilian goods ceased. Millions of women, old people,
and teen-age children went into the factories and fields to replace the able-bodied men who had gone to the armed forces.
Food, clothing, fuel, and medicine went primarily to the fighting
forces, while civilians had to make do with what was left over. In
the cities the population was put under a rigorous ration system
that allocated essential commodities according to the importance
of the work each individual performed for the war effort. Often
the rations could not be supplied because the government simply did not have the resources. Yet despite the hunger, the lack
of medical care, the freezing winter temperatures, and the lack
of fuel for mere civilians, the combined force of patriotism and
the iron military discipline imposed from Moscow sufficed to
keep production going. As the years passed, Soviet output of
guns, artillery, munitions, planes, and tanks rocketed to provide
the weapons needed at the front. The last two columns of Table
2 illustrate the upward trend of output during 1942-1945.

Three circumstances are particularly important in explaining the near miracle of Soviet economic performance during World War II. First, substantial grain and other food reserves had been accumulated precisely for such an ordeal. So, when war broke out, these reserves provided the additional grain to meet minimum bread needs despite the catastrophic decline in farm output. The second factor was the success achieved early in the war in moving hundreds of essential factories, machines, and skilled workers out of threatened western areas into safe regions in the areas east of the Volga. There these factories were reassembled in a matter of months and began contributing again to the country's industrial production. Finally, United States Lend Lease deliveries supplied more than ten billion dollars worth of essential equipment, high protein foods, medicines, and other necessities. In the absence of any one of these three factors, Russia might have collapsed before Hitler's force. Even with all available reserves, the war period was a time of suffering unmatched since the years of civil war and foreign intervention during 1918-1921.

## The Years since World War II

The Soviet Union emerged victorious from World War II, but it had paid a high price. Its human losses were of the order of twenty to thirty million dead with additional millions crippled and maimed. Many of the Soviet people who had survived the war without physical injury were nevertheless exhausted after four years of great toil and deprivation. In the vast western areas which the Nazis had occupied, there was billions of dollars worth of destruction. Great cities and small towns lay in ruins, their factories, power plants, and railroad lines partially or entirely destroyed. In 1945 many foreigners and Soviet citizens alike believed that many decades of work and sacrifice would be required before Russia could fully heal its war-inflicted wounds.

The reality proved quite different from the pessimistic forecasts. The Soviet Union, like France, West Germany, and Japan, recovered from the war relatively quickly, and then went on to heights of economic power never before known in that country. Some figures may help to make the achievement more concrete. Measured in constant 1966 prices, Soviet gross national product in 1945—including both goods and services—was probably in the range of $75-$85 billion. By 1950, it was approximately $132 billion, already significantly above both the 1940 and 1945 levels. By 1960, the comparable figure was above $250 billion; by 1967

Soviet gross national product was probably in the neighborhood of $372 billion. Stated another way, available independent estimates suggest that the Soviet gross national product approximately quadrupled in the twenty-two years after 1945.[15] Similarly, there is warrant in Western estimates and Soviet data for the belief that in the same period after 1945 Soviet industrial production grew a minimum of five-fold, and perhaps even six-fold or more.[16] Agriculture, as might be expected, increased much more slowly. Nevertheless the peak Soviet farm output in 1967 may have been approximately three times the very low agricultural production of 1945.[17] This steady, continued, often rapid economic growth has permitted the Soviet Union to play the role of military, political, and scientific giant on the world scene since 1945.

The rapid Soviet expansion of output after World War II permitted the USSR for a time to reduce the United States production lead, but in the 1960's there has been little change in their relative standings. In 1950, Soviet gross national product was 31.9 per cent that of the United States. By 1961, the ratio had risen to 47.3 per cent, but during 1962-67, total Soviet output varied around 46 to 48 per cent of United States gross national product.

Several main sources of Soviet economic growth since 1945 are immediately evident. First, the Soviet Union has enjoyed a quarter century of domestic tranquillity and international peace. There has been nothing comparable to the struggle over collectivization since World War II, and the costs of the Cold War, while substantial enough, have at the same time been far less

---

[15] These data are mainly taken from or based upon *Soviet Economic Performance: 1966-1967* (Washington: U.S. Government Printing Office, 1968), p. 16, and Stanley H. Cohn, "Soviet Growth Retardation: Trends in Resource Availability and Efficiency," in *New Directions in the Soviet Economy*, Studies prepared for the Subcommittee on Economic Policy of the Joint Economic Committee of Congress of the United States (Washington: U.S. Government Printing Office, 1966), Part II-A, p. 109. The data for 1945 are the author's estimates based upon the Cohn calculations plus the 1944 estimate in Bergson, *op. cit.*

[16] These statements are based primarily upon the data in James H. Noren, "Soviet Industry Trends in Output, Inputs, and Productivity," in *Ibid*, Part II-A, p. 280, as adjusted backward to 1945 and forward to 1967 in the light of heavily discounted official Soviet statements regarding industrial production growth during 1945-1950 and 1965-1967.

[17] This statement is based on rough backward and forward extrapolation, in the light of official Soviet data, of the estimates in Douglas B. Diamond, "Trends in Output, Inputs, and Factor Productivity in Soviet Agriculture," in *Ibid.*, Part II-B, p. 346.

than the price of involvement in any military conflict. The United States, it is worth remembering, has been involved in both the Korean and Vietnam wars during the same period. Second, during both the Stalin and post-Stalin eras, the rulers of the Soviet Union have continued the policy of investing normally more than a quarter of the gross national product annually, and devoting the largest single share of that investment to increasing capacity in mining, manufacturing, and construction. Even as late as 1963-1964, private consumption in the Soviet Union was only 46.5 per cent of the gross national product, the lowest proportion in any of the seven major economies in the world.[18] The historic Soviet policy—common to both the Stalin and post-Stalin periods—of increasing heavy industrial production more rapidly than the output of consumer goods has been the mechanism for implementing emphasis on defense and capital investment. Third, the Soviet government has sought to keep as high a proportion as possible of its able-bodied population at work. Civilian employment in the Soviet Union grew by almost one-half between 1950 and 1968, while civilian non-agricultural employment doubled approximately over the same period. The substantial contribution of increased manpower to increased production has been partially offset since 1956, however, by reductions in the length of the Soviet work day and work week.

A major theme in Soviet planning and public exhortation has been the need to increase productivity of labor and other resources. To achieve it, a variety of means have been employed from the introduction of improved technology to the wide use of incentive payment schemes for workers and peasants. This background makes particularly interesting some unexpected results emerging from research by Moorsteen and Powell. They found that in 1953, the year of Stalin's death, productivity of Soviet resource use was roughly at the level of 1937. This implies that the increasing rigidity and irrationality of Stalin's rule in his later years essentially offset "all gains from improved technology for a period of more than a decade and a half." Put another way, the increase of output during 1937-1953 was primarily the fruit of a massive increase in the amount of resources applied to production. But from 1953 to 1961, the increase in Soviet productivity was rapid, representing apparently "the taking up of slack, as it were, left in the system at the time of Stalin's death."

---

[18] Cohn, *op. cit.*, p. 106.

For the entire period 1928-1961, Moorsteen and Powell conclude that increased input of resources alone accounted for well over one-half and perhaps even three-quarters or more of the increase in Soviet output. These inputs, they note, "were not costs voluntarily incurred but costs imposed upon the population by the exertion of compulsion of the severest sort. In large degree, hence, the rapidity of Soviet growth is a testimonial to the efficacy of authoritarian political controls—a demonstration of the potentialities of 'growth by force.' "[19]

Of the years since World War II, 1945-1950 were the most difficult. The impact of the war's human and material losses was felt most severely during those years. Moreover, Stalin's economic civilian policy, as announced in his February 1946 speech, assumed that war against his recent allies, especially the United States, was likely, and that highest priority must go to preparation for that conflict. We now know that well before the Nazi surrender Stalin had ordered resumption of work on nuclear weapons. This research produced a Soviet atomic bomb by 1949 and a Soviet hydrogen bomb by 1953. Agriculture was starved of capital in those years. Farm produce was extorted from the collectives at confiscatory low prices, while heavy industrial and weapons production again received top priority. The monetary reform of December 1947 was conducted in such a way as to destroy the currency savings of the population and to make it economically imperative for almost every adult who could get a job to do so.

In 1921, Soviet economic conditions had been so bad and Communist party control of the population so shaky that Lenin had found it necessary to make the major retreat that was the New Economic Policy. It is interesting to note that after World War II Stalin made no comparable retreat. Stalin had effective substitutes in 1945 for Lenin's resort to legalized private enterprise. Stalin had a labor army of millions of German, Italian, Japanese, and other prisoners of war whom he could and did use as slave workers. His armies occupied all of Eastern Europe as well as Manchuria and North Korea when World War II ended. This enabled Stalin to loot these areas of billions of dollars worth of machinery, raw materials, farm products, and other valuable goods needed in the Soviet Union itself. Most important, the prestige enjoyed by the Soviet regime because of the victory

---

[19] Richard Moorsteen and Raymond P. Powell, *The Soviet Capital Stock, 1928-1962* (Homewood, Ill.: Richard D. Irwin, Inc. 1966), pp. 288-93.

over Hitler and the tight political control maintained by the secret police assured that the Soviet people did not revolt against their hardships in the early post-war years.

By the time Stalin died in 1953, however, the tensions resulting from the sacrifices he had extorted from the Soviet people made his heirs nervous about the security of their power. From Georgi M. Malenkov to Nikita S. Khrushchev to Leonid I. Brezhnev and Aleksei N. Kosygin, successive post-Stalin rulers have gone to great lengths to assure their people they were aware of popular dissatisfaction with low living standards and intended to improve matters.

As early as August 1953, the then Premier Malenkov told the Soviet people, "It is our pressing task in two or three years to raise sharply the general availability of foodstuffs and manufactured goods . . . to make a substantial increase in the supply to the public of all consumers' goods." He promised an "abundance of food" by 1955 or 1956 and admitted openly that "an acute shortage of housing is felt everywhere."[20] Inevitably, Malenkov's program aroused the opposition of the Soviet military establishment and of the chiefs of Soviet heavy industry, setting off a bitter struggle over priorities in the allocation of Soviet resources. When Malenkov was forced to resign as Premier in early 1955, the victor, Khrushchev, underlined the violence of the conflict over economic policy. Those advocating that growth of consumer goods production should overtake other branches of industry slandered the Communist party, Khrushchev charged. He added, "This is a right deviationist belching, a vomiting of the anti-Leninist ideas which Rykov, Bukharin and their sort once spread."[21]

Yet within a short time Khrushchev also appeared in public as the apostle of a better standard of living for the Soviet people. In effect he took over Malenkov's ideas as Stalin, three decades earlier, had taken over Trotsky's. At the twentieth Communist party Congress in February 1956, Khrushchev repudiated the old Leninist-Stalinist premise that war between Communist and capitalist countries was inevitable. Communism could triumph on the world scene, he argued, by defeating capitalism in a pro-

---

[20] *Pravda*, August 9, 1953.

[21] *Ibid.*, February 3, 1955.

duction race. The implication of this argument, an implication Khrushchev made ever more explicit as time went on, was that ultimately Communism would win by giving the people of Communist-ruled countries a higher standard of living than that enjoyed by the populations of capitalist states. In the months following Khrushchev's enunciation of the new line, much of the old Stalinist system of coercion of Soviet workers was ended, the release of slave laborers from Soviet concentration camps was speeded up, and minimum wages and pensions of Soviet workers were raised. But this was only a beginning. By mid-1957, Khrushchev was assuring the Soviet people that in three or four years they would have as much milk and meat as Americans. "This victory of ours will be stronger than the hydrogen bomb," he exulted, adding, "If we catch up to the United States level of meat, milk and butter we shall have shot a highly powerful torpedo at the underpinnings of capitalism."[22] Like the Malenkov promises which had preceded them, these Khrushchev pledges were not fulfilled on schedule either. But by 1961, Khrushchev had dashed on to his boldest set of promises. That year he unveiled a schedule for reaching the full Communist Utopia, declaring that the Soviet Union would be on the very threshold of realizing Marx's dreams by 1980. The Third Program of the Soviet Communist party, adopted in October 1961, ended with the ringing words: "The Party solemnly proclaims: The present generation of Soviet people will live under Communism!"

Khrushchev's downfall in October 1964 was the result in part of the wide discrepancy between his grandiose promises to Soviet citizens and the more modest results he actually delivered. In the wake of Khrushchev's ouster, *Pravda* denounced "harebrained scheming, immature conclusions and hasty decisions and actions divorced from reality." Khrushchev's flamboyant promises to the Soviet people were undoubtedly examples of the "harebrained scheming" *Pravda* had in mind.

In retrospect, Khrushchev's major single contribution to Soviet economic growth after Stalin was in the field of agriculture. He did secure substantial growth of farm production during the 1953-1958 years. In part, he encouraged higher production by raising

---

[22] *Ibid.*, May 24, 1957.

sharply the prices paid farmers, increasing supplies of farm machinery and fertilizers, and improving agricultural efficiency by abolishing the Machine-Tractor Stations and selling their equipment to the collective farms. He also sponsored a vast increase in the area planted to grain in the so-called "virgin lands" of Siberia and Kazakhstan. But by the early 1960's Khrushchev was unable to get further major gains in farm output. He was forced to impose sharp increases in meat and butter prices in 1962, a measure whose unpopularity helped set the stage for his ouster from power in 1964.

The Brezhnev-Kosygin leadership that followed Khrushchev continued the post-Stalin tradition of assuring the Soviet people of the regime's special solicitude for raising living standards. Thus in presenting the five year plan for 1966-1970 to the twenty-third Soviet Communist party Congress in April 1966, Premier Kosygin told his audience that the party would follow a policy of speeding up the growth of the people's living standards. In words reminiscent of those used by Malenkov in August 1953, Premier Kosygin declared:

> In the course of many years the production of consumer goods has had a growth rate appreciably lower than the output of means of production. The level of development of the national economy which has been attained permits the new five year plan to raise significantly the growth rate of agriculture and bring it closer to the rate of industrial development. And within industry the new five year plan will bring the rate of growth of consumer goods closer to the growth rate of means of production. [23]

In line with this attitude, the new agricultural program announced in March 1965 provided for an unprecedentedly large program of investment in agriculture. Similarly the 1968 economic plan called for consumer goods output to increase more rapidly than production of heavy industry. This was contrary to most past Soviet practice.

The emphasis above on the recurrent failure of post-Stalin Soviet regimes to deliver fully on their repeated promises of rapid improvement in standard of living should not be misinterpreted, however. There was growth in real incomes during these years, even though at a slower pace than promised. An index of per capita Soviet consumption computed by two American scholars

---

[23] *Ibid.*, April 6, 1966.

put the increase between 1950 and 1965 at 82 per cent, while their index of total consumption grew more than 130 per cent in the same period.[24] There could be little doubt that by the late 1960's the Soviet people had the highest standard of living in their history. But that standard was still well below the level of other European industrial countries and much below that of the United States. Moreover, the appetite of the Soviet people for still faster improvement had been repeatedly whetted by their leaders. The contrast between the Soviet Union's ability to land rockets on the moon and on Venus, and its failure to provide automobiles for more than a minute fraction of its people was, inevitably, a source of discontent.

In looking back over the turbulent half century of Soviet economic development, certain lessons seem evident. By creating a totalitarian state and economy, a series of Soviet leaders have succeeded in making their country one of the two great world military-industrial-scientific powers. Their methods have proved far more effective in industry than in agriculture, in part because farm output is heavily dependent upon uncontrollable climatic factors and in part because for many years in the 1930's, 1940's, and early 1950's Soviet farmers had little incentive to produce on the collectivized fields. With the passage of time, the death of Stalin looms as an ever more imposing milestone. His disappearance from the Moscow scene set the stage for dismantling the system of coercion and exploitation that he had created. But though the leaders who succeeded Stalin have felt more compelled than he to make clear their interest in improving living standards, their primary aim in practice has still been to maximize Soviet power through production of the most modern weapons, through expensive space exploits that make useful propaganda, and through economic assistance to and other penetration of underdeveloped non-Communist countries. All this has required and still requires a continued high rate of investment, plus continued, if narrowing, priority for heavy industry. The behind the scenes struggle over division of the Soviet Union's capital resources is undoubtedly a key source of tension in the late 1960's. This struggle arrays against each other leaders of the Soviet military-scientific establishment, the chiefs of heavy in-

[24] David W. Bronson and Barbara S. Severin, "Recent Trends in Consumption and Disposable Money Income in the U.S.S.R.," in *New Directions in the Soviet Economy*, Part II-B, p. 521.

**Chart 1.** Official Soviet Indices of Industrial and Agricultural Output Growth, 1944-1967

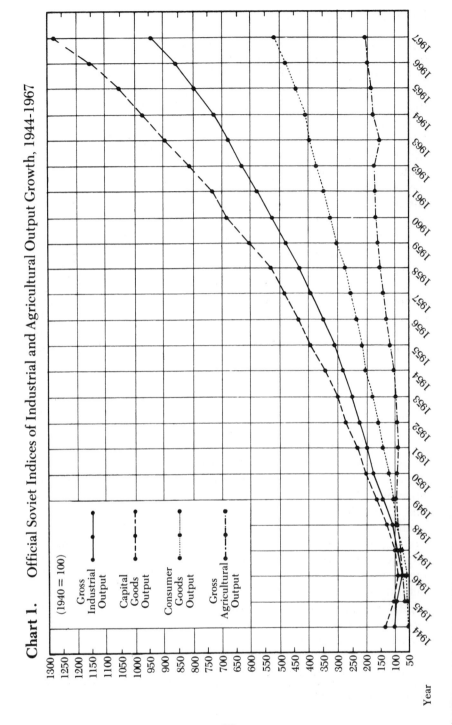

Year

# Chart 2. Soviet Steel Production, 1945-1967 and Soviet Grain Production, 1945-1967

Soviet Grain Production, 1945-1967

Soviet Steel Production, 1945-1967

(million metric tons)

Year

1945 1946 1947 1948 1949 1950 1951 1952 1953 1954 1955 1956 1957 1958 1959 1960 1961 1962 1963 1964 1965 1966 1967

10 20 30 40 50 60 70 80 90 100 110 120 130 140 150 160 170

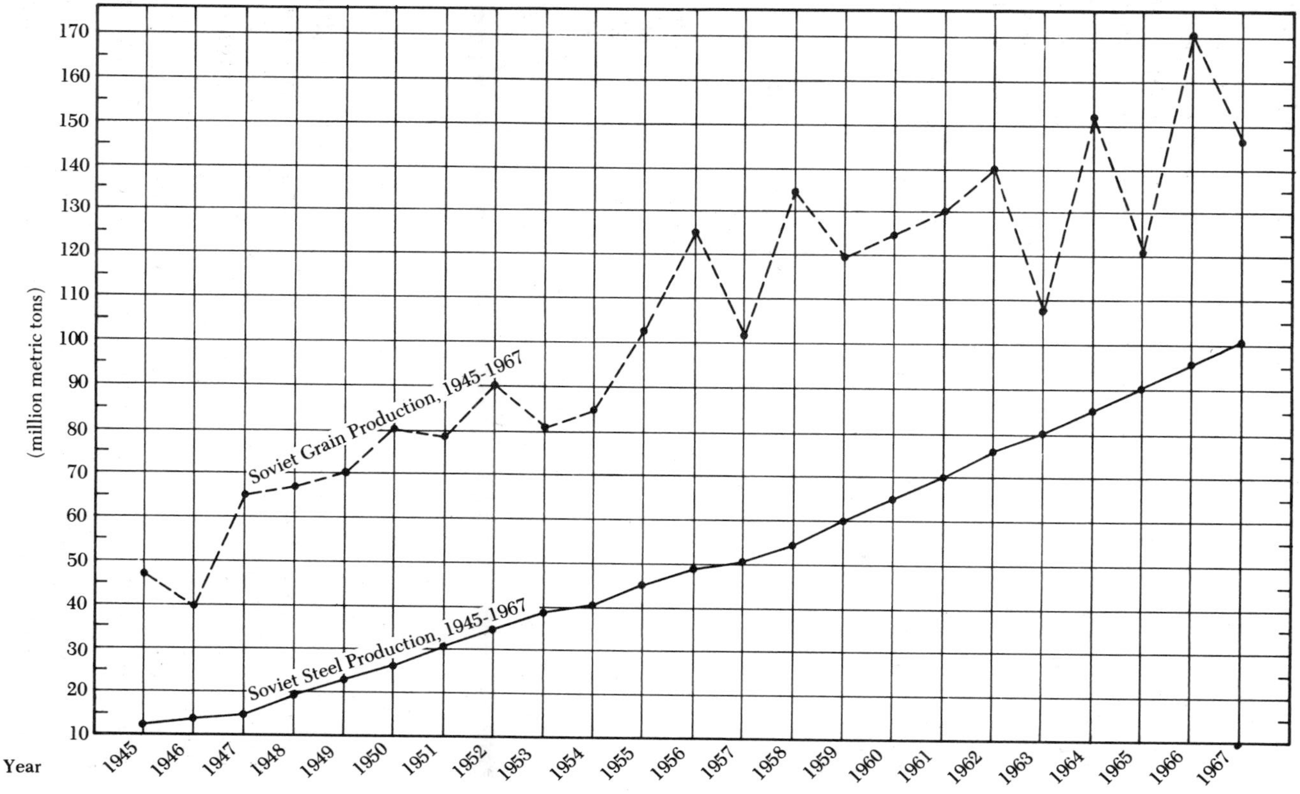

dustry and spokesmen for Soviet consumer goods and agricultural interests.

Yet it is also clear that in the second half of the 1960's the process of departure from the Stalinist economic model is speeding up. The stimuli have been provided by increased popular pressure for better living standards, by concern over repeated setbacks in agriculture and over signs of a declining rate of growth of national income and industrial output, by increasing contact with the non-Communist world and its ideas, and by growing awareness of the suicidal nature of any future thermonuclear conflict.

Table 3 sums up the recent industrial production growth of the Soviet Union, the dynamic force that has so transformed that nation over the past decades.

**Table 3.**    Soviet Production of Key Industrial
Commodities in 1940, 1945, and 1967
and Output Goals for 1970

| Commodity | Unit | 1940 | 1945 | 1967 | 1970 Goal |
|---|---|---|---|---|---|
| Steel | mil. metric tons | 18.3 | 12.3 | 102.2 | 124.0 |
| Coal | mil. metric tons | 165.9 | 149.3 | 595.0 | 650.0° |
| Oil | mil. metric tons | 31.1 | 19.4 | 288.0 | 350.0 |
| Electricity | billion kwh | 48.3 | 43.3 | 589.0 | 801.0 |
| Shoes | million pair | 211.0 | 63.1 | 561.0 | 673.0 |
| Television | million sets | † | — | 5.0 | 7.5-7.7 |

° Partially estimated.
† 300 television sets were produced in 1940.
Sources: *Narkhoz 1965, passim.*, and *Pravda*, April 10, 1966, October 11, 1967, and January 25, 1968.

Table 4 summarizes the complex story of Soviet agricultural production since 1940. The disaster of World War II was followed by a period of very slow improvement during the late 1940's. It was not until Stalin's death in 1953 that the earlier stagnation was broken, and in the remainder of the 1950's farm output grew substantially. Progress slowed once more in the first half of the 1960's, but then in 1966 and 1967 new records in agricultural production were set again. Over the entire period, however, Soviet agricultural production growth was both much more uneven and much slower than were the corresponding gains made in industrial output.

**Table 4.**   Soviet Production of Key Agricultural
Commodities in 1940 and Selected
Later Periods

| Commodity | Unit | 1940 | 1946-1950 Average | 1956-1960 Average | 1966-1970 Average Goals |
|-----------|------|------|-------------------|-------------------|-------------------------|
| Grain | mil. metric tons | 95.5 | 64.8 | 121.5 | 167.0 |
| Cotton | mil. metric tons | 2.2 | 2.3 | 4.4 | 5.6-6 |
| Meat | mil. metric tons | 4.7 | 3.5 | 7.9 | 11.0 |
| Milk | mil. metric tons | 33.6 | 32.3 | 57.2 | 78.0 |
| Eggs | billions | 12.2 | 7.5 | 23.6 | 34.0 |
| Wool | thous. metric tons | 161.0 | 147.0 | 317.0 | ° |

° Not available.
Sources: *Selskoye Khozyaistvo SSSR Statistichesky Sbornik*, pp. 202 and 329.
Kosygin's speech in *Pravda*, April 6, 1966.

The failure of Soviet agriculture in the early 1960's to reach the ambitious goals proclaimed by Nikita S. Khrushchev helped set the stage for his purge in 1964. The Brezhnev-Kosygin program of higher prices for farmers and of greatly expanded investment in agriculture helped to secure the sharply higher farm output of 1966 and 1967. But as 1967 ended there were signs that powerful Soviet interests were arguing for a less generous attitude toward farming, claiming that part of the capital directed to agriculture could be better employed to meet the needs of heavy industry and defense.

# Soviet Population and Natural Resources 2

With a land area roughly two and one-half times that of the United States, the Soviet Union occupies a larger portion of the earth's surface than any other single nation. In large part, the economic progress of this vast country since 1917 has been the result of the disciplined organization of the Soviet people to exploit the great natural wealth available in this enormous land. Not all Soviet resources, however, are equally abundant; some —notably those available for agriculture—are seriously deficient. In this chapter we shall try to examine the magnitude and quality of the human and natural resources available for Soviet economic development.

In 1968, the Soviet Union had about 238,000,000 people, the largest population in its history, spread over the vast expanse of its territory in Europe and Asia. The uneven distribution of this population is indicated by the fact that the European portion of the Soviet Union had over three-fourths of the Soviet people though its area is only about one-quarter of the total. More than 55 per cent of the Soviet population in 1968 lived in cities and towns, a sharp change from earlier periods when most Soviet citizens lived in rural areas. Moscow with about 6,500,000 inhabitants and Leningrad with about 3,700,000 were the largest Soviet cities, but eight other communities had populations of about a million or more: Kiev and Kharkov in the Ukraine, Baku on the Caspian Sea, Tashkent in Central Asia, Gorky and Kuibyshev on the Volga, Novosibirsk in Western Siberia, and Sverdlovsk in the Urals.

Under the impact of wars, famines, and drastic internal political struggles, the population history of the Soviet Union in the twentieth century has had many tragic chapters. On January 1, 1917, the area Lenin later conquered—excluding the areas not conquered until 1939 and afterward—had about 145,000,000 people. Six years later, on January 1, 1923, this area had only about 136,000,000 inhabitants, the decline reflecting the terrible losses of the civil war and famine in the intervening years. Population growth resumed as the NEP restored more normal conditions in the 1920's, but then it slowed down and almost ceased in the first half of the 1930's. The early years of the thirties once again saw famine in the Ukraine and elsewhere, while population increase was also held back by the fierce struggle over collectivization. There was sharp improvement later in that decade and by the beginning of 1939 the Soviet Union had about 170,000,000 people. Taking into account the population in the territories added to the Soviet Union from 1939 until early 1941 (Eastern Poland, the Baltic States, Rumania's Bessarabia and Northern Bukovina) as well as normal population growth, the expanded Soviet Union probably had about 200,000,000 people when Hitler attacked in June 1941. World War II proved a major demographic catastrophe. At its end the Soviet population was down to about 170-175,000,000 people, and the population did not attain its prewar level until 1956, more than a decade after the war's end.

We may sum up half a century of population change by noting that on the constant present territory of the Soviet Union—including all the areas acquired since 1939—there were more than 160,000,000 people in 1917 as compared with 235,000,000 people in 1967. The average annual increase over this period, therefore, was under 1,500,000, less than 1 per cent of the 1917 population.

The population catastrophe of World War II deserves a closer examination since its effects are still being felt in the Soviet economy. Many more Soviet males died during World War II than females, and as a result the country's population has suffered a serious sexual imbalance since 1945. At the beginning of 1950, the Soviet Union had only about 78,000,000 males as against

102,000,000 females. In mid-1967, there were still 19,000,000 more females than males, but the discrepancy was concentrated among those over the age of 35. This has meant, of course, that since World War II many more Soviet women have been without husbands than would have otherwise been the case, and at the same time women have made up the bulk of the Soviet labor force. A second result of World War II was a calamitous decrease in the number of births during 1942-1946 because millions of men in the armed forces were away from their wives. Some data suggest that only one-third as many children were born in 1943 and 1944 as in 1939 and 1940. In the early and mid-1960's, the impact of this demographic blow was felt in the sharply reduced number of persons reaching maturity and entering the labor force. Presumably, this factor was also significant in the precipitous drop in the Soviet marriage rate from 12.1 per thousand in 1960 to only 8.5 and 8.7 per thousand in 1964 and 1965, respectively.

Since migration into or from the Soviet Union has been small during the past two decades, population change has been essentially determined by the balance between births and deaths. Soviet birth rates and death rates, particularly the former, have shown a downward trend in the main since 1950. In that year the Soviet death rate was 9.7 per thousand; in 1967, it was 7.6 per thousand. The decline in the birth rate—from 26.7 per thousand in 1950 to 17.4 per thousand in 1967—has been much more steep. The result has been a slowing down of Soviet population growth, in both absolute and relative terms. During 1958, Soviet statisticians estimate that their country's population increased by almost 4,000,000 people; in 1967, the official estimate put the annual population gain at only about 2,300,000 people or little more than 50 per cent of the increase in 1958. In 1967, moreover, the annual rate of natural population growth fell below 1 per cent for the first year in modern peacetime Soviet history.

The trends of Soviet births and deaths since 1950 have much of their origin in forces common to the advanced industrialized countries, as well as in some forces especially relevant to the Soviet experience. The increasing urbanization of the Soviet Union has tended to reduce birth rates, while improvements in sanitation and medical care have cut death rates. Increased knowledge of contraceptive methods has provided the means for lowering birth rates. A powerful incentive for birth control has been and is the Soviet urban housing shortage and its resultant crowded living conditions. The government prohibition against abortion, in effect from the mid-1930's to mid-1950's, did not eliminate illegal abortions, and in 1955 the Soviet regime lifted the ban. No data on abortions are published, but there is some evidence to suggest that during periods in the 1960's the number of pregnancies ended by abortion may have been greater than the number of live births. The very dramatic 25 per cent decline of the Soviet birth rate in the first half of the 1960's presumably reflects, among other factors, the great reduction in the number of young adults reaching maturity and marrying in those years, another consequence of the sharp decline in births during and immediately after World War II. The low Soviet death rates of the past decade have been somewhat artificial because they reflect in part the absence of older people who died prematurely during World War II rather than surviving to die normally in the 1950's and 1960's. Presumably, Soviet death rates will rise in the future as this abnormality disappears.

The increased urbanization of Soviet population has been the product of its rapid industrialization. In both 1917 and 1926, only 18 per cent of the Soviet people were urbanites. By 1939, there were 63,000,000 dwellers in cities and towns, 33 per cent of the total population. As of mid-1967, the comparable figures were 129,000,000 persons, 55 per cent. Even though somewhat more than half of its population is now urban, the Soviet Union still has an extraordinarily large percentage of rural inhabitants as compared with the other major industrial nations of the world.

A major increase in education and in numbers of trained personnel has accompanied the extensive industrialization and urbanization in the Soviet Union. Total enrollment in schools and training programs jumped from 10,588,000 in 1914-1915 to 47,547,000 in 1940-1941 and to about 65,000,000 in the mid-1960's. The government's huge investment in education and training has given it the most educated and most skilled industrial and agricultural labor force in its history, as well as large numbers of scientists, engineers, architects, and other highly trained professionals. On the other hand, the major shakeups in the Soviet educational system this past decade have reflected dissatisfaction with its operation and a search for improved means of preparing Soviet young people to meet their society's needs for trained manpower.

In a vast country such as the Soviet Union, there are as a matter of course sharp differences in demographic trends among different regions. The disparity between urban and rural birth rates provides one vivid example, as shown in Table 5.

**Table 5.** Soviet Rural and Urban Birth Rates, 1913-1965

| Year | Urban | Rural |
|------|-------|-------|
| | *(births per 1,000 population)* | |
| 1913 | 30.2 | 48.8 |
| 1926 | 34.1 | 46.1 |
| 1940 | 30.5 | 31.5 |
| 1950 | 26.0 | 27.1 |
| 1965 | 16.2 | 21.0 |

In 1965, the Soviet republics in Central Asia with their large rural Moslem populations had birth rates varying from 31 to 37.2 per thousand population. Latvia, on the other hand, had only 13.9 and Estonia only 14.8 births per thousand population. Death rates varied from a low of 4.7 per thousand in Kaliningrad province and 5.8 per thousand in Armenia and Kazakhstan, to 10.6 and 10.1 in Estonia and Latvia. In 1965, the Tadzhik, Turkmen, and Azerbaidzhan republics had natural rates of population increase—i.e., birth rates minus death rates—of 3 per cent annually; Central European Russia, Estonia, and Latvia had natural rates of increase significantly less than one-half of one per cent annually. [1]

## The Raw Material Base

The Soviet Union is extremely rich in raw materials. It has enormous forests whose potential for lumber production is still far from fully exploited. It has numerous swift-flowing rivers— the Volga, the Dnepr, the Ob, and the Lena, among others— that have been and will be tapped for hydroelectric power. Under the surface of its vast territory are major deposits of iron ore, coal, oil, natural gas, bauxite, uranium, diamonds, gold, silver, copper, zinc, lead, and other raw materials essential for modern industry. Moreover, there is every reason to suppose that additional rich resources will be uncovered as prospectors and geologists continue to probe the nation's vast area.

The Soviet Union's great resource wealth does not preclude raw material problems. Some difficulties arise from progressive

[1] This section on Soviet population has been based on *Narkhoz, 1965, passim.,* *SSSR v Tsifrakh v 1967 godu* (Moscow: Tsentralnoye Statisticheskoye Upravleniye, 1968). *passim., New Directions in the Soviet Economy*, Part III, *passim.,* and *Soviet Economic Performance: 1966-67*, pp. 49-63.

exhaustion of the richest mineral deposits which have been worked for many decades at the earliest centers of Russian and Soviet industry and population. This has imposed increased costs as older coal mines have had to be exploited at ever greater depths and as ores with lower iron and other metal content have had to be used. Moreover, much of the Soviet Union's mineral wealth is found in Soviet Asia, relatively far from the present centers of population and production. Great capital investments are needed to develop these deposits. Often they are located in areas with almost no population, with no rail or road connections to other parts of the country, and with very severe, long winters. In these adverse conditions it is extremely expensive to build entire communities from scratch and to provide roads and other necessary infrastructure. It is expensive, too, to move the raw material obtained there to distant centers of consumption. On the other hand, technological progress tends to ease the problems arising from depletion of resources by finding cheaper methods of extracting minerals—for example, strip mining of coal which is extensively employed—and by finding substitute raw materials—for example, the generation of power from uranium fission rather than from conventional fuels.

On January 16, 1967, Pravda described the wealth of Soviet resources and their geographic maldistribution in these words:

> The USSR has approximately 55 per cent of the world reserves of coal, 45 per cent of the natural gas, more than 60 per cent of the peat. It has significant reserves of petroleum. Of the general world quantity of oil-bearing area, 32 million square kilometers, about 11.9 million square kilometers, or 37.1 per cent, are on the territory of the Soviet Union. Only 8 per cent of our potential hydroelectric power resources have so far been utilized. The European part of the USSR and the Urals have most of the population of our country. In these areas are located also the chief potentials of the national economy. But 87 per cent of the mineral fuel reserves are located in Siberia, the Far East and the Central Asian republics. In the eastern regions are found the basic reserves of the economical types of fuel: gas, oil and also more than 90 per cent of the hydroelectric resources.

In the Stalin era, the Soviet fuel economy was dominated by coal. In 1950, coal accounted for about two-thirds of all the caloric content of fuels consumed in the Soviet Union, petroleum for 17 per cent, peat for 5 per cent, wood for 9 per cent, and natural and byproduct gas for 2 per cent. Since Stalin's death great emphasis has been placed upon increasing the relative share of the more economical oil and gas fuels. By 1967 therefore, coal accounted for less than 40 per cent of all Soviet fuel, petroleum for over 37 per cent, gas for over 17 per cent, peat for 2 per cent, and wood for about 3 per cent. [2]

The chief Soviet source of coal is the Donets Basin (Donbas) which produces about one-third the national total, a sharp percentage drop—though not an absolute one—from the 56.8 per cent it provided in 1940. The Kuznetsk Basin (Kuzbas) accounted for another 17 per cent of Soviet coal in the mid-1960's, only little more than in 1940. Other major sources are the Moscow Basin, whose coal is of poor quality, the Pechora Basin northeast of Leningrad in the Arctic, the Karaganda and Ekibastuz Basins in Kazakhstan, a large variety of deposits in the Urals, and miscellaneous coal regions in Eastern Siberia and the Far East. [3]

Before World War II most Soviet oil came from the Baku region on the Caspian, but primacy has long since passed to the Volga-Urals area, called the "second Baku." If the rich oil deposits found in Tyumen Province in western Siberia in recent years are followed by other rich Siberian discoveries, the center

**Table 6.** Distribution of Soviet Petroleum Output in 1966

| Area | Oil Output (million metric tons) | Percentage Growth in 1966 |
|---|---|---|
| Tatar Region | 83.2 | 9 |
| Bashkiria | 46.3 | 6 |
| Kuibyshev Province | 33.7 | 1 |
| Perm Province | 11.5 | 18 |
| Orenburg Province | 3.4 | 31 |
| Tyumen Province | 2.8 | 200 |
| Grozny | 11.2 | 25 |
| Stavropol | 5.1 | 12 |
| Ukraine | 9.0 | 23 |
| Baku | 21.7 | 1 |
| Turkmenistan | 10.7 | 11 |
| Kazakhstan | 3.1 | 54 |
| of which Mangyshlak field | 1.4 | over 300 |
| Belorussia | .2 | over 400 |
| USSR total | 265 | 9 |

Source: *Ekonomicheskaya Gazeta*, No. 17, 1967, p. 36.

[2] *Strana Sovetov za 50 Let* (Moscow: "Statistika," 1967), p. 68.

[3] *Ekonomicheskaya Entsiklopediya Promyshlennost i Stroitelstvo* (1965), III, 522.

of Soviet oil production may well move east of the Urals. The chief sources of Soviet oil in 1966 and their rates of production growth for that year are shown in Table 6.

The flourishing and rapidly expanding Soviet natural gas industry has developed almost entirely during the period since World War II. The major deposits now being exploited are in the Ukraine, in the Volga and North Caucasus areas of European Russia, and in Uzbekistan in Central Asia. Large reserves are also reported to have been found in Tyumen Province in western Siberia, enough, it is claimed, to double the Soviet Union's known gas resources.

Soviet iron and steel production, the core of Soviet heavy industry, has been largely based on the country's rich resources of iron ore and coking coal. The great Ukrainian iron and steel industry grew out of the fortunate proximity of the Donbas, very rich in coking coal, and the iron ore of Krivoi Rog. More recently the poorer quality iron ore of the nearby Kerch peninsula has also been exploited intensively. Even in the 1960's, Krivoi Rog and the Kerch peninsula have provided half or more than half of all Soviet iron ore. In the early 1960's, about a quarter of all Soviet iron ore came from the Urals where the most famous deposit—now seriously depleted—is at Magnitogorsk. The scarcity of coking coal in the Urals induced Stalin to turn to the Kuzbas coal mines in western Siberia. He set up steel plants in both the Urals and the Kuzbas, meeting their raw material needs by long distance rail shipments which brought Kuzbas coal to the Urals and Urals iron ore to the Kuzbas. The advantages, from a military and strategic point of view, of having major steel plants deep in Russia's interior were very much in Stalin's mind when he made these decisions. Later, part of the Kuzbas iron ore needs were met from nearby mines at Gornaya Shoriya. Depletion of the richest iron ores has forced the Soviet Union to turn to poorer quality deposits which must be concentrated and otherwise improved for blast furnace use at significant cost. New sources opened in recent years, are becoming the bases for new major iron and steel production centers. The large iron ore reserves of the Kursk Magnetic Anomaly in central European Russia have received a great deal of attention this past decade, and were providing 13.5 million tons of ore annually in the mid-1960's, despite the difficulties posed by large underground rivers in this region. The deposits in Kazakhstan, particularly at Atasu near the Karaganda coal basin and in Kustanai province have also been vigorously developed. In the more distant future, the Soviet Union will be able to tap the rich iron ore deposits of eastern Siberia, particularly in the Angara River valley and adjoining areas. Economically, of course, it is most advantageous to have supplies of iron ore near the centers of steel production. This consideration explains the priority being given in the late 1960's to expansion of the Kursk Magnetic Anomaly's output. By 1970, iron ore production capacity there is scheduled to reach 31 million tons.

The Soviet Union has numerous deposits of virtually all other major industrial minerals, but limitations of space permit only a brief discussion here. The very important, though little publicized, Soviet aluminum industry is based on extensive deposits of bauxite and other aluminum-containing minerals which are found in many places in both European and Asian Russia. Copper, zinc, lead, and other non-ferrous metals are also found in complex ores at many sites, particularly in the Urals, Kazakhstan, and the Udokan-Chulman region of Eastern Siberia. The chief Soviet sources of uranium appear to be in Uzbekistan in Central Asia and in the Ukraine. The largest sources of Soviet gold production appear to be in the Aldan Plateau and the Kolyma area of eastern Siberia, though there have been recent reports of major gold finds in Uzbekistan and Tadzhikistan. The discovery of extensive Soviet diamond deposits in the Yakutsk region in the early 1950's was a major addition to Soviet assets. Manganese deposits at Nikopol in the Ukraine and Chiatura in Georgia have been important for decades. In general, the Soviet Union maintains strict secrecy about production statistics for almost all metals besides iron and steel. This makes it difficult for foreigners to reach accurate conclusions about the magnitude and adequacy of Soviet output of these materials.

Despite the Soviet Union's undoubted wealth of mineral resources, there has been increasing pressure in recent years for more economical, less wasteful attitudes. In part, this economy move has been precipitated by realization of the cost of developing Siberian resources to replace or supplement older, partially exhausted supply sources. Typical of the current attitude is the August 1967 article in *Literaturnaya Gazeta* complaining of the huge waste of Soviet fuel resources. The author deplores the high loss of coal in underground mining—up to 47.2 per cent in Karaganda—and the fact that only 30 to 40 per cent of available Soviet petroleum is actually pumped from the ground. And he estimates the waste of Soviet natural gas during 1959-1965 as equivalent to 50 million tons of oil or 100 million tons of coal.

## Resources for Agriculture

Most of the Soviet Union is located in the same latitudes as Canada, in a portion of the globe where the chief climatic feature is the great length and severity of the winters. In the extreme northern tundra zone of the Soviet Union, the subsoil is permanently frozen and temperatures rarely rise above the freezing point. Even farther south, particularly in Siberia, the summers are simply too short to permit the growing of conventional crops. Ironically, much of the land in one of the key southern areas of the Soviet Union, Central Asia, is also unusable for agriculture because it is an arid desert. As a result only about 10 per cent of the Soviet Union is used for conventional farming.

Most Soviet agriculture is carried on in what has been called the "fertile triangle," formed very roughly by lines connecting Leningrad in the north, Odessa in the south, and Lake Baikal in Siberia. But even in this most favored region, agriculture has to be pursued against many natural obstacles. Much of the southern portion of the triangle—stretching from the Ukraine to Novosibirsk in Siberia—is a fertile steppe blessed with the famous *chernozem,* or black earth soil. But the rains are undependable in this region. When they come in adequate amounts at the right seasons, the crops are rich. Every few years, however, this zone has little or no rainfall and the crops are very poor.

In central and northern European Russia, the rainfall is more adequate and more dependable. In fact, in some parts of this zone agriculture is actually hampered by large areas of waterlogged and even swampy ground. But the poor quality soil, deficient in many essential plant nutrients, often yields poor harvests.

The effort to overcome these natural limitations has often engaged the attention of Soviet leaders. Back in 1948, Stalin announced a vast program for planting trees over some 15,000,000 acres with the objective of creating a great forest shelterbelt that would shield much of European Russia against the hot drying winds blowing from the deserts east of the Caspian. That project was largely abandoned after Stalin's death. In more recent years, there has been much discussion of and allocation of capital for expanded irrigation in the southern areas (subject to drought) and for reclamation of the swampy lands farther north in European Russia. Recently, too, fertilizer production has been increased to provide the means for improving the fertility of the soil in central and northern European Russia. In earlier periods, expenditures on irrigation and fertilizer were largely concentrated on limited areas capable of producing relatively high value industrial raw materials. Thus irrigation and fertilizers have been important for decades in the Central Asian regions which produce most of the Soviet Union's cotton.

Nikita Khrushchev's ambitious "virgin lands" project that began in the 1950's was another effort to break out of the limitations that natural conditions impose upon Soviet agriculture. In Kazakhstan and adjoining virgin-land areas, tens of millions of acres of semi-arid territory having extremely undependable rainfall were newly planted to grain. More than a decade's experience with the exploitation of these new grain territories has demonstrated above all the sharp variations of production that take place from year to year in response to the sharp fluctuations in moisture supply. The large harvests that have been reaped in the virgin lands in some years, for example 1958 and 1966, have been offset by poor crops in such years as 1963 and 1967. Even the good crop years cannot obscure the fact that a high price is being paid for this land's cultivation. The price takes the form of extensive land erosion—evidenced most spectacularly in periodic dust storms—that is threatening the basic fertility of the precious top soil in this great region.

# Soviet Economic Organization     3

Too much popular discussion of economic systems exaggerates the differences among them. We are all accustomed to hearing about socialism versus capitalism or economic planning versus free enterprise in black-and-white terms as though the contrasting systems had nothing in common. Reality, however, is much more complex. All existing systems are mixed economies. There are major differences among the systems but for the most part these differences result from the varying proportions in which different national economies combine government and private ownership, central planning and grassroots economic decision making.

The confusion on this point explains the recurrent talk about the Soviet Union's becoming capitalist or the United States' turning socialist. If capitalism is properly understood as a system based primarily on the private ownership of land, factories, and other instruments of production, then there is not now and has not been for many years any sign of a Soviet "return to capitalism." What has been taking place, as we shall see below, is a trend toward Soviet adoption of some techniques of economic decision making familiar to the West but, until recently, denounced in the Soviet Union. Soviet economists once derided the utility of competition in the market place and regarded the goal of maximizing profits as immoral and socially harmful. Experience has been causing them to modify these ideas, but this by no means indicates a wish to return to private ownership of most capital. Yugoslavia, after all, has been demonstrating for almost two decades that a socialist society—founded on public ownership—can employ competition, market determination of prices and production, and the profit motive to help improve the performance of its socialist economy.

The most important fact about the Soviet economy is that the Soviet government occupies a monopoly or near monopoly position in many areas. It effectively owns and operates virtually all of Soviet industry, mass transportation, communications, banking, foreign trade, and education and social services, as well as most retail and wholesale trade and much of Soviet agriculture. But the Soviet Union also has a private economic sector which is far from insignificant, especially if account is taken of the large amount of illegal as well as legal private economic activity. Finally there is an important cooperative sector, consisting mainly of collective farms and of an extensive system of rural consumer co-operatives.

Legal private economic activity in the Soviet Union is that which does not violate either of the two basic prohibitions of Soviet law. The first bans private persons from acting as trade middlemen; that is, it forbids the purchase of commodities for resale at a profit. The second prohibits a private person from hiring another for the purpose of making a profit from his employe's work. Thus, a shoemaker may not hire an assistant to help him repair shoes, but a Soviet general may hire a maid or a gardener because the general is not making a profit from the services of such personnel.

Against this background, there are two main legal types of private Soviet economic activity. One is the free market sale of foodstuffs grown by collective farmers and others who have small garden plots. The free markets in which these sales are made have fluctuating prices set by supply and demand. In the second instance, a vast variety of Soviet artisans and professional men—many of whom work for the state during regular working hours—sell their services in their free time. A Soviet city dweller knows that the fastest way to have a television set or a toilet repaired is to employ a private repairman who will do the required work, at a price. Similarly, many Soviet citizens see doctors in the latters' homes and pay a fee, even though the same doctors can be seen without fee in government clinics. Presumably these private patients feel they get more adequate and more attentive service than they get in the clinics. Soviet creative artists—writers, painters, composers, and the like—normally sell their products to state enterprises. Painters and sculptors, however, have the option of selling their work to private Soviet collectors, and some do so.

There are no statistics on the total magnitude of illegal private economic activity in the Soviet Union, but it is undoubtedly vast. The chronic shortage of goods in Soviet cities and towns has made for persistent black markets in which scarce goods are sold at high prices. Black marketeers may be small fry like the scalpers who hawk tickets at the Bolshoi Theatre, or they may be enterprising entrepreneuers who buy up early tomatoes in sunny Georgia and fly them to Moscow for sale at very high prices during the winter season. The boldest and most ingenious souls among these illegal entrepreneurs are big businessmen who at times amass millions of rubles. One Pyotr Borovskoy, for example, went into the business of buying uncut diamonds, sapphires, and rubies that workers had stolen from government plants. He had the precious stones cut to specifications by jewelers and then sold them at handsome profits. His buying agents ranged Russia and one of them, who was caught at an airport, had 409 rubies on his person. Leonid Rulev, a flour mill hand, bought grain at the low state price, paid his fellow workers overtime wages to grind it into flour, and then hired scores of farmers' wives to sell the flour at high prices. Before he was through he had several university professors, a ballet dancer, two retired army generals, and a police officer working for him as flour salesmen.[1] The seriousness with which the Soviet government views such large scale organized private business was revealed a few years ago when the government passed a law instituting the death sentence as punishment for large-scale illegal private business operations.

## The State Sector

The state sector of the Soviet economy is the largest single economic organization in the world. It employed over 85,000,000 people in the late 1960's. It includes factories, mines, banks, in-

---

[1] Gabriel Lorince, "The Underground Millionaire," *New Statesman*, June 2, 1967, p. 755.

surance companies, hospitals, railroads, schools, publishing houses, radio and television stations, department stores, research laboratories, foreign trade firms, farms, and a host of other economic units. Even the largest Western capitalist enterprises—firms like General Motors or the American Telephone and Telegraph Company—are small by comparison with the gigantic size of the Soviet state sector. The number of the Soviet government's industrial plants and mines alone exceeds 200,000, while the number of other types of Soviet government economic units—stores, schools, hospitals, offices for handling postal and other communications, and so forth—runs into additional hundreds of thousands. And this vast agglomeration of human beings and institutions is spread over a nation having an area more than twice the size of the United States.

Inevitably, an organization of this enormous size, complexity, and territorial dispersion poses the most formidable problems of control and integration. The inadequacies of the mechanisms which have been employed to try to run this huge complex have been at the root of many of the ills of the Soviet economy. In retrospect, the surprising thing is perhaps that the unwieldy and clumsy state sector of the Soviet economy has accomplished so much in the way of increasing production and capital investment. Soviet economists now admit that their country's progress has been achieved at enormous and excessive cost and with staggering wastes and inefficiencies. The key theme in Soviet economic thinking in the post-Khrushchev era of the late 1960's is the need to refashion Soviet administration and control so as to eliminate the expensive irrationalities of the past. The effort now is to find means that will give optimal solutions to Soviet economic problems.

The state sector built up under Stalin and continued under Khrushchev was essentially structured on a military principle. The commander of an army in war time has a clear and simple objective: victory over the enemy. He has complete control over the troops under his command and deploys them as he sees fit in order to achieve the objective. In the Soviet economic hierarchy, those in authority at each level until the mid-1960's knew that their task was simply to maximize production along the lines ordered by their superiors. In the Soviet command economy of the Stalin-Khrushchev era, orders flowed from the top to the bottom, and Soviet consumers tended to be regarded as the civilian equivalents of army privates.

Stalin explicitly rejected, though it may be doubted that he ever really understood, an alternative model—one based on market relationships. He associated market coordination of economic life with capitalism and private ownership. His economists often derided what they termed the "anarchy" of market economies. In a market organization, of course, enterprises are governed not by orders from higher authority but by the signals of the market place, primarily the fluctuation of prices, reflecting competition among buyers and sellers. In the simplest models of a market economy, enterprises seek to maximize their profit by producing or increasing the output of those goods whose prices will bring profits and reducing or eliminating the production of goods whose prices bring losses. Stalin disliked the implication of autonomous enterprises implicit in a market system. He had no faith in Adam Smith's idea of competition acting as an "invisible hand" that forces producers to serve the social interest even while they seek primarily to serve their own interests. It was precisely in the Soviet economy's freedom from "wolfish competition" that Stalin saw one of the great virtues of the economic structure he created. Yet, ironically, it was in the late 1920's, when Stalin was fashioning his system, that an American economist, Professor F. M. Taylor, described a technique through which market coordination could be used fruitfully in a socialist economy rather than being exclusively an adjunct of an economy based on private ownership.

Let us look now at the "command economy" Stalin created by following the military analogy. That "command economy" ruled the Soviet state sector virtually unchallenged for three and one-half decades after the late 1920's. It is still dominant in the late 1960's, though radical changes have begun.

The basic unit of Soviet state economic activity is the enterprise. It may be a factory, a division of a railroad line, a newspaper, a television station, a large department store, a uranium mine. Somewhat akin to a Western corporation, a Soviet enterprise is a legal personality that can sue and be sued and that can enter into contractual relations with other enterprises. It has a charter defining its permitted activities. The enterprise also has fixed and working capital provided by the state, which, of course, is its sole owner. The enterprise operates as part of a money economy; it pays its suppliers and workers and is paid in turn by those to whom it sells its production or services. The guiding principle of the enterprise's work is *khozyaistvenny raschet* (us-

ually referred to as *khozraschet*), a term best translated as economic accountability. Put another way, the *khozraschet* principle
requires that a Soviet enterprise behave in many respects like a
Western business enterprise, by using its resources as economically as possible, by being responsible for its debts, and by trying
to make its income exceed its expenditures. The reader will note
that we exclude from consideration those parts of the Soviet
economy which do not normally sell their goods and services,
for example, the Soviet armed forces, the school system, and the
medical care apparatus. Having little or no sales income, these
units are financed by the state through budgetary allocations.[2]

Important as the similarities are, the analogy between a Western business enterprise and a Soviet *khozraschet* enterprise breaks
down at some crucial points. For one, the Soviet enterprise is
not truly autonomous; its director—who is in theory the commander of the enterprise under the Soviet principle of *yedinonachaliye,* or one man rule—has in the past been as much under
the command of higher authority as is the captain of an infantry
company. No less important is the fact that a Soviet enterprise
in the Stalin and Khrushchev eras did not regard as its main objective earning a maximum profit. Rather, its primary objective
was to fulfill or to overfulfill the economic plan's production targets, whether stated in physical terms or in rubles. Thus if a
steel plant was directed to produce 1,000,000 tons of steel in a
given year, its director and other key personnel were praised
and given bonuses if they produced that much or more steel during that year. But if they fell below that goal, they were open
to criticism, demotion, even—in the worst years of the terror
during the 1930's—imprisonment or worse on charges that they
had deliberately sabotaged production. Maximum production
was Stalin's goal. He judged his minions by how well or how
poorly they contributed to this goal, using the plan's targets as
his measuring rod or success indicator.

The problem facing a Soviet enterprise director in the Stalin-
Khrushchev era was much more complex than the preceding para-
graph suggests because his orders from above—his enterprise
plan—covered far more than production targets. Superior authority normally sought to prescribe in advance as many aspects
of his work as possible. He got directives as to how many workers he could hire and how much he could pay them, how much

---

[2] The latest version of the rules governing Soviet state production enterprises
may be found in *Ekonomicheskaya Gazeta,* Oct. 20, 1965, pp. 25-29.

raw material and how many semi-fabricated items he could use per unit of his plant's output, how large an inventory he might maintain of different production essentials and what level of costs would be acceptable. The prices at which an enterprise could sell its products were usually determined by higher authority as were the quantities of key materials it could receive. Little wonder that Soviet enterprise directors generally felt themselves bound hand and foot, forbidden to use their judgment or initiative. For decades the more enterprising among them complained repeatedly, calling for more freedom and scope for independent decision making.

More was involved in these complaints than mere resentment at being treated like children. Enterprise directors knew from their own experience that many of the directives they received were inconsistent with one another and that it was usually impossible to operate their plants exactly as called for by higher authority. Meeting the predetermined unit cost, for example, might make it impossible to produce an item of desired specifications; obedience to government limitations on inventories of raw materials might force the plant to suspend operations when a spell of bad winter weather interrupted rail deliveries; inadequate allocation of essential components for the enterprise's needs might delay or halt production. It must often have seemed to Soviet plant directors that their instructions came from a berserk computer. In late 1965 a Soviet economist explained the situation in these terms:

> What was the basic defect of the systems of planning, management and stimulation existing until recently? It was that the effort to establish from the center all the detailed working conditions for each factory lead inevitably and objectively to a mechanical, equalizing approach. Since it was impossible for the center to know exactly the situation at each enterprise, it operated on the basis of a theoretical average which did not correspond to the actual conditions at any one factory. To this average there was added an approximately equal rate of growth for all, producing assignments which were easy for some enterprises and impossible for others.[3]

Soviet enterprise managers reacted to these difficult conditions in many ways, but the very nature of the system elicited four rather typical responses. First, managers tended to make fulfillment of the production goals the central point of their activity since their

---

[3]A. Birman, "Mysli Posle Plenuma," *Novy Mir*, December 1965, pp. 202-203.

bonuses were dependent on quota fulfillment. In many cases they sought production regardless of cost and, if necessary, sacrificed quality for quantity. At the extreme—though obviously not always—factory activity tended to become production simply for the sake of amassing good statistics that would bring bonuses, regardless of whether the goods produced were wanted or needed by anyone. It was not the factory's worry if its products piled up unsold in warehouses—as happened increasingly in the early 1960's. The factory and its leaders were judged by production, not sales. Inevitably the chase after maximum output often involved violating other plan directives, such as those setting goals for cost reduction or economy in the use of particularly scarce resources. But factory directors knew that there was a good chance they could go unpunished if they were victors in the production race because, as the cynical Soviet proverb says, "Victors are not judged." In 1959, an effort was made to change matters by making many bonuses dependent upon reducing costs to planned levels or even to lower figures, but the evidence suggests that the tremendous inertial force of the production emphasis was little affected by the reform.[4]

In addition, many Soviet managers tended to become highly skilled at deceiving their superiors. A prime goal of every Soviet director was to receive an "easy" plan, one whose production targets he could attain without excessive difficulty. He soon found that the simplest way to receive an easy plan was to hide from superiors the full extent of available productive capacity. Moreover, if a factory failed to achieve its output targets, production statistics could be falsified. Many a manager reported as production in a given period the actual output plus the inventory of finished goods the plant had on hand from earlier periods. Or a plant manager might play fast and loose with the funds allocated to him and use credits assigned for paying wages to finance badly needed factory maintenance. Such violation of financial discipline was disguised by appropriate false bookkeeping entries. Needless to say, the Soviet regime tried to check this deception by maintaining an army of different kinds of inspectors and by punishing individual culprits. Moreover the plant director's superiors often were men who had previously been factory managers. They knew

---

[4] Here and elsewhere in this section the author has drawn upon the pioneering research of Joseph Berliner and David Granick and also upon Barry M. Richman, *Soviet Management with Significant American Comparisons* (Englewood Cliffs, N. J.: Prentice-Hall, 1965), Chapter 8.

the standard tricks and tried to make appropriate allowances for such questionable activities. But these superiors also had a stake in the good performance of the enterprises they supervised.

In other instances, Soviet managers tried to fulfull their output plans in the easiest way possible by adjusting the assortment of products they turned out to take advantage of the way in which the targets were stated. If a factory's plan was stated in terms of a total ruble output goal, the manager would try to produce as many as possible of his most expensive item even though this would result in a deficiency of the less expensive items. If his plan called for manufacturing a certain number of units, conversely, he would seek to favor production of the simplest and most easily manufactured items. And if the goal was stated in terms of weight, managers emphasized production of the heaviest items. Nikita Khrushchev's 1959 complaints about these abuses are worth reproducing:

> It has become traditional to produce the heaviest chandeliers possible rather than just beautiful chandeliers to adorn homes. This is because the heavier the chandeliers manufactured, the more a factory gets since its output is figured in tons. So the plants produce chandeliers weighing hundreds of kilograms and fulfill the plan. But who needs such a plan? . . .
> Furniture factories have plans stated in rubles. Hence they find it best to make a massive armchair since the heavier the chair the more expensive it is. Formally the plan is fulfilled since the furniture makers add various details to the armchair and make it more expensive. But who needs such armchairs? . . . Everybody knows this. Everybody talks a good deal about this, but still the armchairs win. [5]

Further, Soviet managers over the years developed great virtuosity in finding informal (illegal) means of coping with shortages that threatened their output goals. Shortages arose either because the plan had not allocated sufficient materials or workers or because the supplies had failed to arrive at the plant on time. One way of offsetting such problems was to hoard materials or workers or both, and to disguise the hoarding by bookkeeping manipulations. If a factory produced complex machinery requiring many parts, it tended to try to make as many of those parts as possible itself in order to reduce its dependence on untrustworthy suppliers. The factory's cost of production of these parts, of course, was much higher than that of the specialized suppliers. Finally,

---

[5] *Pravda*, July 2, 1959.

a factory in difficulties could and often did try to get help. It might turn to the local Communist party boss to exert influence to get needed deliveries; or it might send a *tolkach,* an envoy, to other plants to try to get the needed materials. The most talented and enterprising of the *tolkach* breed were, in effect, major independent businessmen having commissions from many factories. They often had contacts that permitted them to arrange complicated deals in which different factories exchanged their surplus supplies in order to remedy their deficits. A factory director might also use his *blat,* or influence, to solve his problems by calling for help from officials who were old friends or for whom he had done illegal favors earlier. All these informal activities were, of course, at gross variance with the economic plan and with Soviet law. Their justification was that they permitted the adjustments without which many factories could not fulfill their output targets.

Thus the reality of the Soviet economic apparatus even in the worst Stalinist days, let alone in the more relaxed Khrushchev period, was a complex union of the planned and the unplanned. Little of the Soviet economy corresponded to the beautifully articulated machine purring along smoothly according to an ideal plan; much of it was an incredible melange of many clashing gears, square pegs in round holes, and great internal friction. Essentially, two factors made it operate: the absolute priority of production, and the ability of the human beings who manned the Soviet economic machine to make innumerable informal adjustments that served the cause of production when the plan and its execution broke down.

The system operated, but at high cost. Much that was produced was little needed or of poor quality, while real and even urgent needs went unsatisfied. Resources were used inefficiently; far less was obtained from the inputs of the Soviet economy than could have been gotten from more rational arrangements. Costs of production were often needlessly high. These problems were often overlooked in the earlier years of Soviet economic development. In those early years the Soviet Union had vast unused resources permitting rapid production growth to be achieved by massive increases of inputs. At that time, too, the Soviet people accepted passively the deprivations to which Stalin's industrialization program subjected them. But by the late 1950's and early 1960's, growth began to show alarming signs of slowing down. It also became clear that the country could not continue to increase indefinitely the inputs of capital, labor, and other resources. Moreover, the political situation was different after Stalin's terroristic methods of rule were abolished. Stalin's successors had to seek the consent of those they governed by putting ever greater stress on improved living standards. As the pressures on Soviet resources increased so did the pressures for greater efficiency in the use of those resources. Inevitably, the search began for improved methods of managing the Soviet economy.

Many alternatives were proposed and debated in the vigorous public Soviet discussion of the problem that was begun by Professor Yevsei Liberman's seminal article in *Pravda* in September 1962. The debate ranged between two extremes. One extreme wished to emulate the Yugoslav socialist market economy with maximum autonomy for enterprises, prices determined by supply and demand, and minimum central planning. The other extreme proposed to introduce a more rational all-embracing central planning system based on mathematical models of the Soviet economy. Electronic computers would hold the vast amount of required information and make the enormous number of computations required by this solution of the problem. Neither extreme offered a realistic answer to the economy's problems. There were too many vested interests in the Soviet central planning apparatus and too much suspicion of the "capitalist" market mechanism to make the Yugoslav example attractive, especially since the Yugoslavs had had enough economic difficulties to show that their model was not perfect. Similarly, it was clear to all except a few enthusiasts that even modern electronic computers and the highly developed methods of mathematical economics—linear and nonlinear programming, input-output analysis and the like—were not capable of handling the information and decision making in so large and complex an economy as that of the Soviet Union.[6]

## The Economic Reform of 1965

The major economic reform announced by Premier Kosygin in September 1965 represented a compromise among many different points of view. It retained the system of centralized planning and decision making on all important issues. At the same

---

[6] For a fuller discussion of some of these alternatives see Egon Neuberger, "Libermanism, Computomania, and Visible Hand: The Question of Informational Efficiency," *American Economic Review*, May 1966, pp. 131-44. A summary of the debate is given in Jere L. Felker, *Soviet Economic Controversies* (Cambridge: The M.I.T. Press, 1966), Chapters 3 and 4.

time, it sought to give industrial enterprises greater freedom of choice, greater maneuverability in use of resources, and increased incentive to operate more rationally and efficiently.

In discussing the economic reform shortly after its adoption, Professor Liberman enunciated as "one of the most important principles of socialist economics," an idea very reminiscent of Adam Smith's "invisible hand" justification for free competition: "That which is advantageous to society must become advantageous to each enterprise, to each of its workers." He saw the new system as leading to an increase in the resources available for consumption because it would permit an increase in the effectiveness of capital investment. This last was a reference to one of the most serious problems prompting the reform, the accumulation of evidence that return per unit of capital being invested in the Soviet economy was declining, implying that more and more capital would have to be invested to insure a given amount or rate of production growth. Against this background, we may summarize the key features of the economic reform as applied to Soviet industry.[7]

1. The rights of enterprises to manage their own affairs and plan their own production activities were widened substantially. This was accomplished by reducing drastically the number of plan directives imposed by higher authority. The most important plan target of the Stalin-Khrushchev era—the gross value of output—was eliminated altogether. Instead, two new plan targets were emphasized for each enterprise: the planned volume of sales and the planned profits, the latter expressed both in absolute terms and as a rate of return on invested capital. The emphasis on sales introduced the feedback feature missing in the former concentration on production. Under the reform, an enterprise is no longer rewarded for producing goods unless and until they can be sold. Hence the enterprise must be far more concerned with turning out goods that will meet customers' demands than was true earlier. The emphasis on profits is intended to motivate enterprises to seek the fullest and most economical use of their resources. The other plan directives listed by Kosygin included direct production goals for the most important commodities, the size of the total wage fund available to each enterprise, the magnitude of each enterprise's payments to and receipts from the state

---

[7] The Liberman article was in *Pravda*, November 21, 1965. The summary of the new economic system is based upon Kosygin's speech in *Pravda*, September 28, 1965.

budget, the volume of central capital investments assigned to the enterprise and its plan for putting new production capacities into operation, the enterprise's assignments for putting new technology into use, and allocations of supplies of the scarcest materials.

2. To increase incentives for good work, the formerly very limited system of Soviet profit sharing—based on the so-called enterprise fund—was greatly improved and expanded. Two special funds were set up for profit sharing purposes. One, the material incentive fund, is derived from the firm's profits and used to pay bonuses for good work during each year, as well as end-of-year bonuses based in part on each worker's length of service. A similar fund for social and cultural measures and for housing construction will permit enterprises to use part of their profits to improve their personnel's living conditions. These profit sharing arrangements attempt to discourage enterprises from hiding their resources to get the easiest possible plan, a practice discussed in previous pages. Under the new system, fulfillment of an enterprise's profit and sales plans will bring relatively greater bonuses than overfulfillment under the old plan and it is hoped that these additional benefits will induce enterprises to seek the highest possible plan assignments that they can reasonably hope to attain.

3. A great many miscellaneous measures in the reform seek to increase each enterprise's freedom of action and its incentives to use its resources economically. Thus the new system encourages direct relations between buyers and sellers as well as market research and informative advertising, but it frowns on mechanical distribution of goods by higher authority. At the same time an effort has been made to strengthen economic relations among firms by increasing penalties for late deliveries, tardy payment for goods, and other violations of contracts. The earlier arrangements for handling capital investments in the Soviet economy are also being changed drastically by the reform, primarily in three ways. (1) New government long-term capital investments will be repayable long-term loans on which interest will be charged. Hitherto such investments have been financed by the state budget as financial grants, carrying neither interest nor obligation to repay. The innovation is to be introduced slowly, starting with capital investments in existing plants and in projects whose costs can be recouped quickly. (2) Enterprises covered by the reform will have to pay interest—initially 6 per cent annually for most enterprises—on their existing fixed and working capital. In the

past, the absence of such interest on capital tended to encourage extravagant and inefficient use of capital, and to induce enterprises to try to get as much capital from the state as possible. The initial 6 per cent interest rate is hardly an economic one since the relative capital scarcity in the Soviet Union would probably justify a much higher rate; nevertheless, even this step represents a significant beginning. (3) Enterprises, which formerly had only limited possibilities for independent capital investment, will have those possibilities increased by creation of the Fund for the Development of Production. This will be formed in part by allocation from enterprise profits and in part by permitting each enterprise to retain a portion of its depreciation charges. But even with such funds available, enterprises wishing to use them will still face the problem of trying to get the materials, machinery, and labor required for such capital investments. The availability of funds does not guarantee that physical resources can be acquired.

Under this new system a Soviet enterprise has, at least in theory, three main paths to follow to improve its performance, and hence to raise the flow of bonuses to its managers and ordinary workers. It can seek to increase its production and sales by using advertising, market research, and similar techniques of Western business. But this alternative is open only if the enterprise can get additional needed materials and labor to meet unsatisfied demand for its production, and this possibility is often foreclosed by higher authority. There is no reason to suppose, for example, that Moscow planners intend to let managers of Soviet automobile plants have the resources needed to expand passenger car production to the limit of existing demand. Many branches of Soviet industry are in the very same position. The head of the Soviet grain combine industry noted in May 1967 that his plants have "almost no conditions for increasing the volume of sales over established plans. There are different causes, but primarily the limitation of material-technical resources." [8]

A second way to improve performance is to produce a higher quality product that can be sold at a higher price. Here enterprise managers must weigh the higher price of a better product against the higher cost of producing it and against the temporary reduction of production that the changeover may require. Finally, the enterprise can attempt to reduce costs. Here a major bat-

---

[8] *Ekonomicheskaya Gazeta*, No. 21, May 1967, p. 11.

tle front has been opened between enterprise managers and part of their labor force. In many Soviet enterprises, productivity could easily be improved, costs reduced, and profits increased if surplus workers were fired. It is still not clear how much power Soviet managers will have to reduce their work force. In effect, the effort to do this creates a clash between the interests of those who would be fired and those who would remain working in the plant and would receive bonuses from the higher profits made possible by the reduction of labor costs. Of course this is not the only way in which costs could be reduced. Many Soviet plants, for example, have small, high cost shops for producing parts that can be turned out much more cheaply by plants specializing in those parts. The temptation will be stronger under the new reform to abandon this high cost local output and to buy from specialized plants. But the check on such a trend will be fear that the specialized plants will not deliver the needed parts on schedule, thus threatening the customer enterprises' production schedules.

This discussion could be continued, but the basic point is clear: Soviet enterprises will have more freedom with the economic reform, but much central planning will remain. Soviet enterprises will still be far more limited than their Western counterparts in their possibilities for initiative. Soviet plants still cannot set their own prices, decide to whom they will or will not sell, decide on radical changes in their product mix, etc. The "new freedom" in Soviet economic life is real but very limited.

Moreover, it will be many years before most Soviet managers have either the education or the experience for much greater managerial freedom. Traditionally, most Soviet executives have been engineers with little economic background. During the debates of 1962-1965, much opposition to the proposed reform came from old line executives who feared that they would be unable to meet the new demands. It should be noted, however, that an intensive program has been underway for several years to train Soviet managers in business administration.

There is yet a further complication. The use of profits as an index of efficiency in the new system assumes that the prices which define the alternatives available to Soviet enterprise managers correctly reflect relative scarcities and costs in the Soviet economy. Soviet economists recognize that this has not been the case. In the past, for example, Soviet prices have normally included no allowance for interest on capital or rent on land. Nor have these prices fluctuated in response to changing demand. The Soviet price system of the mid-1960's and earlier was consequently a very bad guide for economic decisions. Realization of this fact spurred preparation of the comprehensive reform of Soviet wholesale prices introduced in July 1967. But even at the time Soviet officials recognized that much more work was necessary to make the nation's price system a satisfactory guide to rational economic decision making. There were official predictions then that a second extensive price reform would have to be introduced by 1970 or 1971.

Despite these and other problems, Soviet leaders have been introducing the economic reform ever more widely, aiming at universal coverage of the Soviet economy by the end of 1968. Though experimental use of this system had begun even before 1965, the first major steps were taken in 1966 when more than 700 enterprises were transferred from the old to the new arrangements. These employed more than a million persons. By November 1967, 5,700 industrial enterprises producing about one-third of all output were operating under the new system. By mid-1968, 11,000 industrial enterprises accounting for about half of Soviet industrial output were working under the new rules. In 1967, too, intermediate administrative organizations—for example, the Chief Administrations of the Watch Industry, of Combine Construction, and of Margarine Production—began to be shifted to the new economic system.[9] Let us turn, therefore, to the superstructure of the Soviet industrial administrative system.

## The State Sector's Superstructure

Ultimate economic as well as political power in the Soviet Union belongs to those who rule the Soviet Communist party. Stalin, in his day, alone largely set Soviet economic policy, and Khrushchev had very important, though less complete, power over the Soviet economy at the height of his career. In the Brezhnev-Kosygin period, supreme power seems to reside in the Communist party's Politburo. This is aided by an extensive economic control and supervisory force which makes up an important portion of the apparatus of the Communist party's Central Committee. In addition, every important Soviet enterprise has a Communist party unit among its workers and executives. But much of

---

[9] *Ekonomicheskaya Gazeta*, No. 14, April 1967, p. 9, and No. 32, August 1967, p. 1.

the Communist party control is exercised through the formal economic management superstructure of the Soviet state. That state superstructure is headed by the Premier of the Soviet Union and by the Council of Ministers of which he is Chairman.

The state economic management apparatus has changed radically over the decades. In the 1920's and early 1930's, the Supreme Economic Council directed much of the state-owned economy, especially industry. Then, for about a quarter of a century until 1957, the key management agencies were economic ministries, vertical organizations normally ruling all enterprises in a particular branch of production. These ministries were divided into all-union ministries which exercised direct control over an industry throughout the country, and union-republic ministries which delegated much power and responsibility to subordinate ministries in each of what are now the fifteen Soviet republics. Then, from 1957 to 1965, most of the ministries—and the organization by industries they represented—were abolished. Instead, a new system of geographic management was carried on through regional Councils of the National Economy (*sovnarkhozy*), initially set up so that in most cases there was one *sovnarkhoz* in each Soviet province. A *sovnarkhoz* had managerial authority over most of the industrial enterprises—steel plants, coal mines, electric power stations, machinery factories, hosiery mills, etc.—in its assigned geographic area. Then in September 1965, at the time the economic reform was adopted, the *sovnarkhozy* were scrapped and the ministerial organization was reinstituted.

In our discussion of the tactics used by enterprises to evade the crippling limitations of orders from higher authority, it was implicit that Soviet economic organizations have a life of their own. They have goals they seek to attain even if this means departure from the norms and rules of the Soviet state as a whole. The history of Soviet economic management shows that independent life and autonomous goals also characterize the agencies above the enterprise level. This has been the origin of much of the turmoil that produced the changes in the 1950's and 1960's. Ministries and *sovnarkhozy* alike have been accused of putting their own narrow interests ahead of those of the economy as a whole, with consequent injury to a smoothly operating total Soviet economy.

A typical ministry tends to be a large bureaucratic empire encompassing all possible aspects of the industry or economic field over which it has authority. Traditionally it has directed production, controlled the plans of its enterprises, and managed the

flow of goods into and out of the ministry as well as within it. It
has also conducted research, trained specialists in its area, set personnel policies, published relevant books and professional jour-
nals, supervised the construction of housing and other facilities
for workers at its plants, decided issues of technological policy,
and fought for the interests of its industry in Soviet government
councils. The minister in the past ruled his ministry and its subordinate organs with the same kind of *yedinonachaliye* (one-man
rule) power that the enterprise director has over his subordinates.
Quite clearly these sweeping customary ministerial powers clash
with the spirit and the letter of the economic management reform of September 1965. But it is still not clear how severely the
traditional powers will be limited. A leading theme in the dis-
cussions about the future of the ministries, however, has been
the idea that they too will become *khozraschet* organizations
and presumably, too, will have their success or failure measured
by their performance on sales and profits. A Soviet study has
even suggested that relations between ministries and their subordinate organizations be governed by contracts giving each side
rights and obligations. This would attempt to end the situation in
which the ministry has only rights and the enterprise only obligations.[10] But as this is written the ministry is still clearly dominant, and the enterprise must submit its proposed plans to higher
ministerial officials for approval or for rejection and change,
sometimes with little attention paid to the intended greater
freedom for enterprises. In addition, the new charter defining
the rights and obligations of Soviet ministries, adopted on July
10, 1967, states many of the functions and duties of these organizations in a manner reminiscent of the pre-1957 period. Radical
change for the ministries is presumably a matter for the future,
if ever. [11]

A ministry's links with its subordinate organization may be of
several kinds. They may be based on territorial division of the
country into regions or on a functional subdivision of the plants
within the ministry's empire. The intermediate link between
the ministry and the enterprise may be a Chief Administration
(*Glavk*, plural *Glavki*), a sort of subministry. It may be a trust,

---

[10] A. E. Zholkevich *et al.*, *Ekonomichesky Manevr i Metody Khozyaistvo-
vaniya* (Moscow: Ekonomika, 1966), pp. 82-83.

[11] Cf. the text of this charter in *Ekonomicheskaya Gazeta*, No. 34, August
1967, pp. 7-9.

or, a recent development, a branch production association or firm. The last type have been formed in recent years by combining small enterprises engaged in related work—perhaps a series of small shoe factories in one city or a textile mill, a dye plant, and several clothing factories in a given area—into a much larger multi-plant enterprise that can spur specialization and more efficient use of resources.

When the ministries were abolished in 1957, the then Premier Khrushchev accused them of many faults: their huge size and the concentration of power in the central headquarters in Moscow made them too far removed from the grassroots. Many wrong decisions resulted because the decision makers were ignorant of the realities at the production site. The ministries followed policies aimed primarily at their own self-aggrandizement, put departmental interests ahead of national interests, and tried to make themselves as independent as possible of the rest of the economy by needlessly duplicating facilities and services on a huge scale. The classic anecdote tells of two fleets, each belonging to a different ministry, on a river in Russia. One fleet's boats go up river full and down river empty; the other fleet's boats go up river empty and down river loaded.[12]

The *sovnarkhozy*, which succeeded the ministries, did bring responsible decision makers closer to the grassroots throughout the country, but they also brought new problems with them. One was *mestnichestvo*, or localitis, the tendency to put the interests of each particular *sovnarkhoz's* area ahead of the national interest. A typical practice was to satisfy first local needs for a scarce product produced in the area even though government plans ordered that priority be given customers in other provinces. A second difficulty arose from the absence of any powerful functional links among plants in the same industry but in different areas. Faced by similar problems, plants in different regions would adopt different technological solutions, thus imposing needless complications and costs on their customers. A good deal of tinkering was done with the *sovnarkhoz* system in the early 1960's. New coordinating bodies were created in Moscow and the republic capitals; the number of *sovnarkhozy* was cut so that each covered a larger area; state production committees were set up to try to formulate unified national technological policies. But it was all in

---

[12] For a fuller discussion see Harry Schwartz, *The Soviet Economy Since Stalin* (Philadelphia: J. B. Lippincott Co., 1965), pp. 86-91.

vain. Less than a year after Khrushchev's downfall the whole *sovnarkhoz* system was abolished and the ministries reinstated. The intention clearly was to give the ministries a new and more limited role, since they would have to operate within the very different environment created by the economic management reform announced at the same time as the restoration of the ministerial system.

Let us turn now to a consideration of the Soviet economic administration superstructure, excluding agricultural agencies, as it existed in the years immediately following 1966.[13]

Within the Council of Ministers are ten major agencies having responsibilities and power over all or most of the Soviet economy. These ten agencies are listed and explained in the following paragraphs.

The State Planning Committee (*Gosplan*) is the central planning agency, charged with drawing up the annual and five year plans.

The State Committee for Material and Technical Supply (*Gossnab*) controls the distribution of the most scarce materials and machines, allocating them to different uses and users. In 1968 this organization did business with over 86,000 enterprises and accounted for more than 60 per cent of all Soviet wholesale trade in industrial products.

The State Committee for Science and Technology directs research and development work in the Soviet economy.

The State Committee for Construction Affairs (*Gosstroi*) controls almost all major construction projects in the Soviet Union and is influential in the determination of investment policy.

The People's Control Committee is a comprehensive inspection and audit agency which checks Soviet economic agencies.

The State Labor and Wages Committee sets wage rates, production norms, and overall personnel policy for the entire state sector.

The State Committee for Vocational and Technical Education is primarily concerned with training skilled and semi-skilled workers.

The State Committee for Foreign Economic Relations directs the Soviet programs of economic and technical aid abroad.

The U.S.S.R. State Bank (*Gosbank*) is a central financial institution of the Soviet economy with important inspection as well as banking functions.

---

[13] *Pravda*, August 4, 1966.

The Central Statistical Administration is charged with collecting, analyzing, and presenting comprehensive data on all aspects of Soviet economic life.

The numerous ministries listed below have titles that are self-explanatory, except for the Ministry of Medium Machine Building which is really the Soviet Atomic Energy Commission. Most of these ministries are union-republic ministries. The chief exceptions are the military production and machinery industries. Their very centralized control from Moscow was defended in 1965 by Premier Kosygin on the ground that they require "single technical guidance on a countrywide scale to effect the standardization, unification and normalization of units and parts and to ensure their high quality at the modern level of world science and technology." The list of ministries involved in economic management as of mid-1968 follows:

Aviation Industry
Foreign Trade
Civil Aviation
Merchant Marine
Defense Industry
General Machine Building
Transportation
Radio Industry
Machine Tool and Tool
    Industry
Shipbuilding Industry
Tractor and Farm Machinery
Transport Construction
Heavy, Power and Transport
    Machine Building
Electrical Equipment
Public Health
Culture
Land Reclamation and Water
    Resources
Installation and Specialized
    Construction Work
Food Industry
Building Materials Industry
Communications
Coal
Finance
Non-Ferrous Metallurgy

Motor Vehicle Industry
Medical Industry
Gas Industry
Machine Building for Light
    Industry, Food Industry
    and Household Appliances
Instrument Making, Means of
    Automation-Control Systems
Medium Machine Building
Machine Building for
    Construction, Road Building
    and Civil Engineering
Chemical and Petroleum
    Machine Building
Electronics Industry
Geology
Light Industry
Lumber, Pulp and Paper
    and Wood Processing
Meat and Dairy Industry
Petroleum Extraction
Petroleum Refining and
    Petrochemicals
Fishing Industry
Trade
Chemicals
Ferrous Metallurgy
Power and Electrification

The large number of these ministries reflects Soviet belief that most efficient management is obtained when a ministry has a relatively homogeneous group of activities to supervise. At times in the past, for example immediately after Stalin's death in 1953, there have been many fewer ministries. Presumably in the future the number and jurisdictions of ministries will fluctuate in response to the growth of the Soviet economy. The experience gained in ministerial activity under the radically different conditions of the 1965 economic reform will also affect the future organization of this vast apparatus.

Let us conclude this section by discussing briefly the beginnings that have been made in converting the intermediate links of the administrative apparatus—the chief administrations or *glavki*—to the new system of economic management. During 1966 and 1967 this problem assumed ever greater urgency as more and more enterprises made the shift. The urgency arose from the fact that enterprises increasingly found their newly granted independence and autonomy infringed upon by detailed orders sent down by the *glavki* which often seemed to act as though nothing had changed. The reason, it turned out, was that the latter organizations were still operating on the basis of the old system—judgment by the criterion of production plan fulfillment—while their subordinate enterprises had been shifted to the new criteria based on sales and profits! The interference from above was particularly galling for enterprises when the *glavki* ordered changes—say in a plant's production schedule—without making corresponding changes in other aspects of the plant's plan, with the result that the enterprise suffered losses. Beginning with the 1968 economic plan, Soviet national targets were scheduled to be stated in terms of sales rather than output. This presumably will help eliminate the source of friction discussed above. [14]

Two early experiments seeking to adapt these intermediate organizations to the new economic system involved the Chief Administration for Grain Combine Construction and the "Sigma" branch production association which combined various Lithuanian factories and design bureaus engaged in production of scientific instruments. [15] While details of the two arrangements differ, the essential elements are similar. In both cases the administrative organization was given its own independent funds, obtained by taking stated percentages of the profits and

---

[14] *Ekonomicheskaya Gazeta*, No. 20, May 1967, p. 36 and No. 34, August 1967, p. 13.

[15] *Ibid.*, and *Pravda*, February 14, 1967.

amortization allowances of the subordinate factories. With these funds, the administrative organization could accomplish a number of goals. For one thing, when it changed the production schedule of a subordinate unit, it could give monetary compensation for the losses caused thereby. Moreover, the *glavk* could provide bonuses for plant workers who had done especially complicated or especially important tasks well. Thus the administrative organization had financial incentives to offer to induce its subordinate units to follow its instructions. Finally these new centralized funds provided means for giving bonuses to the administrative agency's own workers in a manner similar to the system for providing bonuses to enterprise workers. Thus in the case of the Chief Administration for Grain Combine Construction, bonuses for its specialists were determined by the success of the entire Chief Administration in fulfilling the plans for sales, profits, and production of basic goods. An interesting innovation pioneered by the Sigma organization was the creation of a "Council of Directors," formed of the heads and other key officials of subordinate units and charged with the responsibility for distributing the centralized funds available to Sigma.

These intermediate administrative agencies perform many important functions. They have the power to redistribute an industry's production assignments among different factories if unexpected developments cut a plant's capacity; similarly, they may redistribute raw materials among plants. They engage in technical research and introduce advances made in one factory in all factories, and they are responsible for advertising and accounting on an industry level. [16]

Near the end of 1967, a major Soviet economist summarized some of the key problems that two years of experience with the economic reform had exposed:

> The objective difficulties arise from the fact that the new system has not been worked out in sufficient detail. Thus, for instance, it is becoming obvious that some methods for bringing material pressure to bear on such important organs of economic management as the USSR State Planning Committee, . . . the Ministry of Finance, the banks and the State Committee on Labor are necessary. Indeed, these organs predetermine all the conditions for the operation of enterprises. A mistake in drawing up the plan or in the process of financing can be fatal to a whole project. Hence, somebody must be responsible for these

---

[16]*Ekonomicheskaya Gazeta*, No. 9, March 1967, p. 20, and No. 21, May 1967, p. 11.

errors, somebody has to cover the loss. During the 50 years of operation of the Soviet system of economic management, however, there has been no instance of an enterprise bringing an action against a countrywide economic management body. It is therefore not surprising that such proposals evoke surprise and suspicion . . .

As far as subjective difficulties are concerned, what we have in mind are old habits of economic management which, as experience shows, are not simple to get rid of . . .

To shift from the present system of centralized rationed material and technical supplies to direct wholesale trade of the means of production is an intricate problem . . . It stands to reason that the market for diverse types of the means of production is saturated to a different degree. At a time when some types are in sufficient supply (and there is even a surplus in some lines), others are, to a greater or lesser degree, in short supply. A simple shift to the wholesale trade of the means of production, i.e., scrapping all sorts of stockpiles and transforming the network for material and technical supplies into ordinary wholesale trade establishments would mean that a part of the means of production in short supply could go to less important enterprises and branches.

Incidentally, we have no intention of abandoning—nor should we—the policy of giving priority to certain industrial branches for a given period. And it does not necessarily have to be iron or steel or machine building: It could, in a given five-year period, be the textile or shoemaking industries. It is the principle we are concerned with. How, in conditions of a shortage of a number of means of production and the operation of plant equipment at full capacity, is it possible to combine free trade of the means of production, on the one hand, and priority for one or another branch of economic activity, on the other? As yet neither theory nor practice has the answer. We cannot use the experience of capitalist countries where surplus machinery, raw materials and manpower as well as the possibility of manipulating prices makes the problem easier to solve. [17]

## The Organization of Soviet Agriculture

Since the late 1920's, agriculture has usually been the most laggard area of Soviet production. Even since Stalin's death, the very good years with high harvests—such as 1956, 1958, 1964, and 1966—have frequently been offset by years of stagnant or even sharply declining farm output. In both 1963 and 1965 the

---

[17]A. L. Birman, "Fifth Decade: Economy on the Upgrade," *Soviet Life,* Oct. 1967, pp. 63-64.

Soviet Government was forced to make very large purchases of grain from Western countries in order to meet its food needs.

Part of the blame for these difficulties must be put on the unfavorable climatic and other natural conditions under which Soviet agriculture operates. The amount of rainfall in key periods is still the major determinant of whether the Soviet Union has a good or a poor harvest. But, as Soviet leaders have increasingly recognized since Stalin's death, much of the blame for their agriculture's unsatisfactory performance must be put on its institutional organization and inadequate incentives. Stalin's forced collectivization of Soviet farmers was followed by two decades of ruthless exploitation. The Soviet regime impoverished the collective farms by taking much of their output at prices far below the producers' production costs. Agriculture as a whole was starved of needed investment resources. The dangers in this situation, particularly in its great lack of incentives for production, were recognized shortly after Stalin's death. The corrective measures taken by Khrushchev in the 1950's—higher prices, increased capital investment, the plowing up and sowing of tens of millions of acres in the semi-arid virgin lands territory in Kazakhstan and Siberia—had substantial positive effects for a time in raising output. But by the early 1960's, Soviet farm output was stagnant again and Khrushchev's efforts to improve matters by frequent and improvised administrative reorganizations helped little or not at all.[18] Six months after Khrushchev's ouster, in March 1965, Leonid Brezhnev outlined a comprehensive new farm policy designed to improve the situation radically. It stressed increased prices for farm products and massive capital investments in agriculture. The aim was to restore production incentives and to repair fully the ravages of previous decades of neglect of Soviet farming's capital needs. Even earlier, in the days immediately following Khrushchev's dismissal, his successors had moved swiftly to ease the latter's unwise restrictions on Soviet private farming. The concessions were tacit admissions that the small garden plots of Soviet collective farmers could make larger contributions to the country's deficient food supply if they were permitted to do so.

Soviet agriculture has undergone enormous institutional changes since the first years after World War II. Their magnitude and direction may best be understood by comparing the situation at the beginning of 1950 with that in the mid-1960's. In early 1950, the Soviet Union had about 254,000 collective farms. These

---

[18] The history of this important period is summarized in Schwartz, *The Soviet Economy Since Stalin*, pp. 159-75.

had about 20,000,000 member peasant families who cultivated altogether about 121,000,000 hectares. In that year these *kolkhozy* accounted for 80-90 per cent of Soviet grain, sugar beet, cotton and other major crop production, as well as for about 20 per cent of Soviet meat and milk production. At the beginning of 1968, however, there were only 36,200 *kolkhozy*. These included only 15,400,000 peasant families who worked about 110,000,000 hectares of collective farm sown area. In 1966 the collective farms produced only about 51 per cent of all Soviet grain, though they still accounted for 80-90 per cent of sugar beet and cotton production, and about one-third of all meat and milk. These changes were the result of a policy of amalgamating small collective farms into large ones and also, to a lesser extent, of converting small and poor collective farms into state farms. The average collective farm at the beginning of 1950 had fewer than 100 families and only about 500 hectares of cultivated land. Its counterpart in the mid-1960's had over 400 families—usually spread over a number of separate villages—and almost 3,000 hectares of cultivated land.

In early 1950 the collective farms owned virtually no tractors, combines, or other farm machinery. For the services of such equipment they were dependent upon the government-owned and-operated Machine Tractor Stations, some 8,000 in number. In the mid-1960's, these MTS were gone—having been liquidated in 1958—and the collective farms owned and operated their own machinery. A new government organization, the All-Union Farm Machinery Association (*Soyuzselkhoztekhnika*), acted as a sales agent connecting the farm machinery producers and their *kolkhoz* customers. The Association also provided facilities for major farm machinery repairs to supplement the facilities available on the *kolkhozy*.

In 1950 the Soviet Union had about 5,000 government-owned and-operated state farms. They employed about 2,000,000 workers and had a total sown area of almost 13,000,000 hectares. In 1967 there were over 12,773 state farms employing more than 7,500,000 workers and cultivating well over 85,000,000 hectares. The average state farm in 1967 was a large enterprise with 618 workers employed on a sown area of 6,900 hectares. The vast expansion of the state farm system over this period was mainly the result of the decision in the mid-1950's to use this form of organization on the tens of millions of hectares of virgin land put into production in that period. In 1966, as a result, state farms accounted for 47 per cent of all Soviet grain production as compared with only 11 per cent in 1950.

The private sector of Soviet agriculture shrank between 1950 and 1964, but it was still quite significant in the mid-1960's. In 1950 the private gardens of collective farmers, state farm workers, and other Soviet citizens had occupied 9,370,000 hectares; in 1966 this area was down to 6,800,000 hectares, about 3 per cent of the total sown area. But even in 1966 these private farming activities accounted for 64 per cent of all Soviet potatoes, 42 per cent of all Soviet vegetables, about 40 per cent of all Soviet meat and milk, and 66 per cent of all Soviet eggs.[19]

In theory, the collective farm is a voluntary cooperative organization, independent of the Soviet state and operated on a democratic basis with major policy issues decided by vote of the members. The members elect a chairman, who is the directing head of the *kolkhoz*, and other officials. The labor force of the collective farm is divided into brigades of 50 to 100 or more workers. Each brigade is assigned responsibility for cultivating a section of the farm's acreage or tending some portion of its livestock. The income of collective farmers, until 1966, was a share in the *kolkhoz's* residual income, that is, what remained after production expenses, required contributions to the farm's capital funds, taxes, and the like had been deducted from gross income. Until 1966, the residual income available for paying collective farmers was usually divided among them in proportion to the number of work days each had earned. A work day was an arbitrary unit of labor performance in terms of which a collective farm valued a day's work at different kinds of jobs. The collective farmers' receipts from the *kolkhoz* have normally been partly in cash and partly in produce, meat, grain, and milk.

In general, the democracy of the typical collective farm has been a myth. Collective farm officials have been chosen by local Communist party or Government officials, with approval by the farms' members a mere formality. Similarly these same party and Government officials have been accustomed to going over each collective farm's plans and revising them as they saw fit. In this respect the nominally independent collective farms have often had as little independence as state-owned industrial enterprises. Recurrent efforts were made in the 1950's and early 1960's to give the collective farms and their officials greater autonomy. The dismal verdict on these efforts is implicit in Leonid Brezhnev's complaint voiced in March 1965:

---

[19] The data in this section have been drawn from *SSSR v Tsifrakh v 1966 godu, SSSR v Tsifrakh v 1967 godu*, and *Vestnik Statistiki*, No. 7, 1967, pp. 2 and 90.

We may not ignore the fact that in many cases the democratic bases of the collective farm structure are being rudely violated. In a series of *kolkhozy* the basic mass of the members actually find themselves excluded from consideration of the chief problems of the cooperative's economy.[20]

But even more than lack of democracy, the *kolkhozy* have been plagued by their low incomes which in turn resulted in little or no payment to their members. While he was premier, Nikita Khrushchev declared that prices paid the collective farms in the Stalin era "were so low that the collective farms could not even cover their production expenses from the returns for the sale of their output. The labor of the majority of the collective farmers was practically not paid for . . . Many collective farms for years did not pay even a single kopek for a work day."[21]

The prices paid the collective farms by the state were raised during the Khrushchev era and this improved matters, but the income of most collective farmers continued to be relatively low. At the March 1965 meeting of the Central Committee, the Communist party chief of Pskov Province pointed out that in his region the average monthly earnings of an able-bodied collective farmer were only 29 rubles 20 kopeks as compared with similar averages of 54 rubles for state farm workers and 83 rubles for industrial workers. He warned that these differentials were producing a flight from the farms and declared that if this continued there would be no able-bodied collective farmers left in his province by 1975.[22] Even though Pskov gets some of the lowest agricultural yields in the Soviet Union because of its poor soil, nevertheless the general picture of collective farmers' relatively low earnings sketched above was typical of much, probably most, of the Soviet Union.

The inability of the collective farms to pay satisfactory earnings persuaded those who could to flee, but it also had important repercussions on those who stayed in the countryside. The farm workers found that they could earn much more by utilizing their energies on their private gardens whose produce could be sold at

---

[20] *Plenum Tsentralnogo Komiteta Kommunisticheskoi Parti Sovetskogo Soyuza 24-26 Marta 1965 goda Stenograficheski Otchet* (Moscow: Izdatelstvo Politicheskoi Literatury, 1965), p. 28.

[21] *Pravda*, March 7, 1964.

[22] *Plenum Tsentralnogo Komiteta*, pp. 142-43.

the high prices of the free markets than by working on the collective fields. This sparked tensions. Collective farmers sought to spend as much time as possible on their private gardens, while the state sought to coerce them to devote their time primarily to the collective fields and livestock. Laws were passed compelling collective farmers to spend an ever greater number of days each year working for the *kolkhoz*. Khrushchev, in the last years of his rule, exerted increasing pressure to cut down the size of private garden plots and the number of livestock that could be raised on them. But all these measures produced resentment which did not encourage energetic and efficient labor by those subject to this coercion.

Khrushchev recognized this situation before he was ousted and sought to remedy one grievance of the collective farmers, their lack of a comprehensive social security system such as government employes enjoyed. But the old-age pension system instituted at the beginning of 1965 paid each beneficiary only 14 rubles monthly as compared with an urban worker's minimum 30 rubles monthly pension.[23] A much more radical step to improve the situation of collective farmers was taken in May 1966. This took the form of a "recommendation"—actually an order—of the Communist party and the Soviet state that the collective farms, beginning July 1, 1966, pay their members guaranteed monthly wages based on the rates of pay for corresponding groups of state farm workers. The "recommendation" also advised the collective farms that payments to their members should have first priority on the farms' income, rather than be a residual after all other costs and obligations have been met. To help the many farms which could not afford to pay their members such relatively high earnings, the Government ordered the State Bank to provide five year loans to make possible payment of the higher rates. Presumably this is a calculated gamble that the incentive effected by the higher collective farm payments will be so great that the resulting increased production will more than pay for the added cost. Whether or not this gamble is successful, however, the step represented an historic turning point in the saga of Soviet agriculture.[24]

In late 1967, however, a ranking Politburo member, Dmitry Polyansky, made it clear publicly that the goal of equalizing earn-

---

[23] Schwartz, *The Soviet Economy Since Stalin*, p. 174.

[24] *Pravda*, May 18, 1966. Cf. also the detailed regulations for this in *Ekonomicheskaya Gazeta*, No. 32, August 1966.

ings of state and collective farmers had not yet been reached, in part because of opposition by some officials. He wrote in October 1967:

> It must be admitted that on many *kolkhozy* the payments for the work of collective farm workers is still below that on *sovkhozy* . . .
>
> Economic analysis indicates that earnings from the labor of collective farmers can be increased on all *kolkhozy* to the level of earnings of state farm workers within the very next few years. The shift to guaranteed payment, similar to that in state enterprises, will facilitate bringing the amount of collective farmers' earnings close to that of industrial workers, while the incomes of both rise.
>
> Guaranteed earnings for the collective farmers' work ensures their increasing interest in the results of their labor. Stable earnings in communal production must, of course, be grounded in rising labor productivity and encourage the all around prosperity of the farms. Workers in some agencies, unfortunately, still fail to understand this. Even some State Bank executives have repeatedly tried to discourage the introduction of guaranteed payment to collective farmers and have hindered the granting of credits for such payment. Only political near-sightedness can explain such actions. [25]

State farms are government enterprises operated in many respects on principles similar to government factories. State farms have not operated on full *khozraschet*, however, because the combination of their own inefficiency and low government prices for farm produce have made many state farms chronic deficit operations requiring government subsidy. They had "planned losses" which grew so great in the last part of the Stalin era that Stalin, shortly before his death, wanted to abolish the state farms and turn their lands over to collective farms.[26] Khrushchev expanded the state farm system enormously during his reign, but he too failed to make the farms consistently profitable. Commenting on the state farms in March 1965, Brezhnev complained of their continued losses and of the excessive regulation of their activities from above. He recommended giving state farm directors more scope for decision making and more opportunity to use such profits as they made for bonuses and for the needs of their farms. The goal, Brezhnev said, was to put the state farms on a full

[25] *Kommunist*, No. 15, October 1967.
[26] *Pravda*, March 7, 1964.

*khozraschet* basis, that is, to make them economically independent and profitable. [27]

Two years after Brezhnev's speech, the first major step was taken to put the state farms on a new economic basis. As an experiment, 390 state farms were transferred to full economic accountability under new arrangements very reminiscent of the earlier economic reform in industry. It was indicated that if the experiment succeeded, all other state farms would gradually follow suit.

The key features of the experimental arrangement announced on April 15, 1967 included the following:

1. Participating state farms will be paid the higher prices received by collective farms for produce sold the state.

2. The number of plan directives given state farm directors by higher authority will be cut drastically. The retained directives include: the volume of sales by crop or other product; the total permissible wage fund; the total sum of profits, budget allocations and the charge for fixed farm production assets; the total volume of centralized capital investment; and the volume of deliveries of tractors, farm machinery, fertilizers, and other production supplies allocated by higher organizations. All other indices in the affected state farms' plans will be worked out by those enterprises themselves.

3. State farms put under full *khozraschet* will, with some exceptions, pay the state annually 1 per cent of the value of fixed production assets, excluding however the value of livestock and perennial plantings.

4. Profits of these state farms will be allocated as follows: 15 per cent of planned profit—and 7.5 to 15 per cent of above plan profits—to a fund for material incentives, which may not, however, exceed 12 per cent of the wage fund; 10 per cent to the fund for social cultural measures and housing construction; 20 per cent to insurance; 10 per cent to the fund for strengthening and expanding the farm. The remaining profit can be used for bonuses and for other farm needs. [28]

Presumably the 390 agricultural enterprises in the experiment were largely or entirely strong enterprises, already making a profit and judged most likely to use the increased freedom of economic maneuver constructively. A *Pravda* review of the experiment in

---

[27] *Otchet Tsentralnogo Komiteta*, pp. 28-29.
[28] *Pravda*, April 15, 1967.

late 1967 was enthusiastic about the initial results but noted some problems. For example, successful state farms that were rapidly increasing their profits were faced by the danger they might not be able to purchase needed material resources with these profits. [29]

Ideas more radical than those tried in the state farm experiment are under discussion by economists concerned with the reform of Soviet agricultural organization. One major set of proposals argues in effect for wiping out central planning of farm production and farm procurements and relying on the price mechanism to equalize supply and demand of farm products. Economist G. Lisichkin, for example, has suggested that the state, after deciding how much of a particular crop it will require, announce the price it is prepared to pay for that product. He then continues:

> By increasing (or reducing) the price it is possible to raise (or contract) the area devoted to producing this commodity. Every *kolkhoz* or *sovkhoz* compares the price thus set against its own circumstances and decides whether it can successfully carry on production in these conditions. Then the state will collect offers from the collective and state farms for the sale of the commodity whose output is most advantageous for the farm at the price that has been set and in the given conditions. By comparing the total thus obtained with the total needed by society, it would be possible to plan measures that would bring them together. [30]

Politburo member Dmitry Polyansky has attacked "economists who urge that primacy be given to the market and to commodity relations, free from centralized planning of purchases of agricultural products" and has warned against "unleashing market anarchy." But nevertheless such ideas are circulating, and their day may come. [31]

Finally, we may note that the central administration of Soviet agriculture was altered often and radically in the late 1950's and early 1960's; since Khruschev's removal in 1964 it seems to have stabilized, at least temporarily. As of mid-1968, the key agency is the Ministry of Agriculture, which controls most state farms, supervises the collective farms, and directs farm research. Another, the Ministry of Land Reclamation and Water Resources, is

[29] *Pravda*, Nov. 20, 1967.
[30] *Novy Mir*, No. 2, February 1967.
[31] *Kommunist*, No. 15, October 1967.

charged with executing the large irrigation and land drainage programs adopted by the May 1966 Central Committee plenum dealing with this topic. The State Procurements Committee, as its name suggests, is the agency which manages the purchase of farm produce in the countryside and its delivery to processing and distributing agencies.

# The Soviet Planning and Price Systems
## 4

Economic planning, as practiced in the Soviet Union this past half century or more, has many different roots in the past. Some are in the earlier Socialist literature, both of the Marxists and of the Utopian Socialists. When Lenin took power in 1917, it was already an article of his faith that he would institute a planned economy. But he soon came up against the embarrassing fact that neither Marx nor Engels had ever given a blueprint for detailed economic planning in a socialist society, and, accordingly, Lenin and his colleagues looked for ideas elsewhere. They were attracted by the economic planning practices that Imperial Germany and the United States had used during World War I. In the early years of the Soviet regime, in fact, several efforts were made to hire Bernard M. Baruch—former head of the War Industries Board—so that he might use the experience gained in directing the American economy during 1917-1918 for the benefit of the Soviet economy. Another important source of ideas was a professor at the University of Berlin, Karl Ballod. As early as 1898 Ballod had published a book, *Der Zukunftstaat* (The Future State), intended to remedy Marx's lack of a planning technique. He sought to show "how a centrally planned socialist economy can be organized and what technical means it has to use in order to achieve the great improvement in living standards predicted by Marx." Lenin hailed Ballod's work as a "scientific plan of a socialist transformation of the whole German economy." A modern economist must disagree with that evaluation, but Ballod's ideas had profound impact upon the Soviet Union. More than a few of his ideas were implemented there.[1]

As early as 1920, a committee of experts prepared—at Lenin's request— the so-called GOELRO plan. This set forth goals for the electrification and industrialization of Russia over the next ten or fifteen years. The State Planning Committee, or *Gosplan,* was set up early in 1921. In the mid-1920's this committee produced several sets of annual Control figures which were essentially efforts to forecast the probable development of the Soviet economy over the year ahead. Only with the First Five Year Plan, promulgated in 1928, did the effort begin in earnest to use planning as an all-embracing means of coordinating and directing economic life. In this conception, planning consisted primarily of the issuance of orders from above as to which goods should be produced and in what quantities, where production should be carried on, how the nation's output should be distributed and similar matters. The First, Second and Third Five Year Plans were formulated and implemented between 1928 and the Nazi attack of June 1941, although the war prevented completion of the last plan. After the victory, the Fourth, Fifth, and Sixth Five Year Plans were put into effect beginning in 1946. But the Sixth Five Year Plan had been so poorly drawn up that it had to be abandoned in 1957, and it was followed by a special Seven Year Plan during 1959-1965. The plan for 1966-1970 is now customarily referred to in Soviet sources as the Eighth Five Year Plan. In addition to five year plans, moreover, the Soviet Union has had much experience with annual plans and with special plans of varied duration for particular purposes. Long range plans have not been neglected. In 1946 Stalin outlined the essentials of what amounted to a 15 year plan, while in 1961 the 22nd Soviet Communist party Congress adopted what was in effect a 20 year plan for creating the economic prerequisites for a Communist society by the early 1980's

There was a time when Soviet writers discussed their plans in lyrical terms, implying that the planners had perfect knowledge and could foresee all and control all. Stalin, of course, never had

---

[1] Leon Smolinsky, "Planning Without Theory 1917-1967," *Survey,* July, 1967, p. 118.

such illusions. We have already quoted Khrushchev's revealing comment about Stalin's contempt for the detailed Soviet plans. To Stalin, the bright goals included in each plan were useful to lift popular morale, while the plans themselves were indispensable for channeling resources toward accomplishment of his top-priority goals. He had no compunction, however, about changing plans in mid-course, and he kept up constant pressure for overfulfillment of planned production goals.

The discussion among Soviet economists that resulted in the 1965 economic reform revealed much disillusionment with traditional detailed Soviet economic planning. Here is the way one Soviet economist put the matter:

> Until recently the USSR *Gosplan* distributed centrally 18,000 means of production. In addition, central sales and other agencies distributed tens of thousands of different materials, instruments, etc. The center sent down to lower echelons approved indexes regarding the numbers of enterprises' workers and (in a series of cases) the magnitudes of average wages, as well as norms for working capital and tens of other indexes. But was this actually economically based scientific planning? Or was this a combination of efforts that had developed over decades to try, with the help of small administrative levers, to observe the work of each enterprise and regulate its activities? . . . All of us agree that it is necessary to strengthen centralized planning. But does this mean that, say, in the year 2000 there will be centralized distribution not of 18,000 individual basic materials, but, say, of 40,000 or 400,000? Or perhaps, on the contrary, the success of scientific central planning will consist in the fact that, let us suppose, in the year 2000 not one kind of basic material will be directly distributed by the central planning organs? [2]

The economist's discussion made evident that his hopes were for the latter alternative: the end of detailed direction and planning from above.

Similarly, the entire spirit of the economic reform of September 1965 implies that Soviet economic planning should concentrate on the central variables of the economy, not on details. The Directives for the 1966-1970 economic plan adopted at the 23rd Soviet Communist party Congress in April 1966 specifically ordered that central economic planning focus on major issues. It listed the following key tasks: improvement of the basic national economic proportions, bettering the location of production and promoting

---

[2] A. Birman, "Mysli Posle Plenuma," *Novy Mir*, December 1965, p. 209.

the comprehensive development of major regions, working out and implementing a unified national policy on technical progress, capital investment, wages, prices, profits, finances and credits, and securing high output and deliveries of key products. The Directives also call for "gradual conversion to planned distribution of equipment, materials and semi-finished goods by means of wholesale trade," that is, by means of conventional purchase and sale rather than by direct allocation to specific recipients. Ultimately the hope expressed in Soviet sources is that the economy will be able to operate on what is called "a full *khozraschet* basis." Put another way, the hope seems to be that the Soviet Union will ultimately have a system of prices and other economic instruments so that each manager acting to maximize his enterprise's profits will simultaneously be acting in the fashion required to realize the overall plans of higher authority. But that situation is distant, if it is ever realized at all. Soviet planning in the future is likely to include much of the old as well as the influence of the new. Evolution, not revolution, seems ahead in this area.

At the heart of traditional Soviet economic planning has been the effort to prescribe for a given period ahead—usually a year or five years—how the country's resources should be utilized and for what purposes and in what amounts. Such a plan orders production of a particular pattern of output, by commodities and quantities, during a future period. It also attempts to assure the realization of these orders by prescribing how resources will be distributed among rival claimants and alternative uses. The basic decisions underlying a given plan are laid down by the political rulers of the Soviet Union. These include such matters as the amount of increase in national income to be sought in a given time, the division of that income between investment and consumption, the top-priority production targets, and key issues in Soviet international economic relations, such as the amount of economic aid to be offered other countries. Against the background of these political directives, Soviet planners allocate labor, capital, and other resources. They also seek to assure financial stability by drawing up cash and credit plans designed to equalize the flow of money claims and of goods and services available to meet them. The planners make key decisions about needed capital investment projects, the introduction of major technological innovations, and the schedules of exports and imports over the period in question. The annual plans prepared each year are, of course, much more detailed than the relatively general five year plans.

The preparation of a national plan alone is not enough. The national targets and allocations must be broken down by geographical areas and by government agencies. Then they must be disaggregated still further until each economic unit—factory, farm, government bureau,—at the grassroots has its own detailed plan specifying what it must do during this time and what key resources will be available to it to perform its assignments. The enormity of the task thus attempted is evident.

Historically, the chief goal of Soviet planning has been to facilitate the most rapid possible growth of the Soviet state's military-economic power. The highest priorities in Soviet planning, consequently, have normally gone to military production and to capital investment in heavy industry. In the years since the mid-1950's, high priorities have also gone to the Soviet space effort and to the politically sensitive program of foreign economic aid. But an even more radical change in this same period has been the higher relative importance attached to the needs of consumer goods industry, agriculture, and housing construction. Since 1953 these three areas have been treated much less cavalierly than was customary during the Stalin era.

Work on a Soviet plan proceeds in two directions, from the top down and from the bottom up. Thus, the enterprises and other basic units of the Soviet economy prepare their own proposed plans for a given period ahead. These are submitted to higher authority which combines the plans of similar units, revises them, and sends them still further up the planning ladder. The most important Soviet planning decisions, of course, are made at the top of the planning hierarchy and much grassroots planning has little effect in reality. In practice, the *Gosplan* at the national (Moscow) and republic levels begins broad planning even before it receives the proposals from lower levels. Later, it revises its own plans to some extent in the light of the data received from subordinate echelons. When the final plans are approved at the national and republic levels, they travel all the way down the hierarchical ladder and are broken down by ministries and other operating agencies into plans for the basic production units. Depending upon decisions at higher echelons, there might or might not be much similarity between the original plan drawn up by a particular factory and the plan the factory finally received as the set of orders it had to carry out. A factor that lightened the work load in all this bureaucratic activity was the fact that each year's plan was to a large extent based on the data regarding performance in previous years. As many Soviet complaints have indicated, much planning was simply the assignment of fixed percentage increases in production and fixed percentage decreases in assigned costs of output.

Once the desired quantities of main products have been determined, *Gosplan* economists draw up the main body of the economic plan by using what they call the method of material balances. A balance is an equation. In this case, the left side of the balance consists of the estimated supply during a given time of a particular important product, say a type of steel or electrolytic zinc or natural rubber or any one of a host of other raw materials and fabricated products. The right side of the equation consists of the allocation of this expected supply among all anticipated uses and users of the commodity during the plan period.

The supply side of the equation is basically the sum of three elements: (a) the expected inventory available at the beginning of the period; (b) planned production of the commodity during the period; and (c) imports of the commodity, if any, during the period.

Likewise, the allocation side of the balance equation consists basically of three elements: (a) allowance for inventory desired at the end of the planning period; (b) allowance for anticipated exports, if any, during the period; and (c) the allocations made to the individual user agencies engaged in production, or construction, and distribution. The allocations, in turn, are derived from the production targets of the user agencies. This is done by multiplying the volume of planned production of each product by direct input norms of materials for that product. Thus if the tractor industry is scheduled to produce 10,000 tractors each of which requires 2 tons of steel, 100 lb. of iron, and 10 lb. of copper, the balance for steel will allocate the tractor industry 20,000 tons of steel (10,000 x 2 tons); the iron balance will allocate the tractor industry 1,000,000 lb. of iron (10,000 x 100 lb.); and the copper balance will allocate the tractor industry 100,000 lb. of copper (10,000 x 10 lb.).

A typical balance equation will therefore have this form:

$$S_{io} + P_i + I_i = S_{ie} + E_i + A_{i1} + A_{i2} + A_{i3} \ldots + A_{in}.$$

Here the subscript $i$ identifies the particular commodity; $S_{io}$ and $S_{ie}$ refer to the stocks of inventories at the beginning and end of the period; $I$ and $E$ are imports and exports respectively; $P$ is the annual production; and the $A_{i1}$ to $A_{in}$ are the allocations of the *i*th commodity to each of the *n* user agencies. Depending upon the number of commodities being allocated, the complete plan will have hundreds or thousands of these balance equations.

It takes little reflection to realize the complexity and difficulty of the task of setting up even a minimally satisfactory set of balance equations. For example, the first efforts to do so must inevitably result in finding that the planned supply of some commodities is much less than the allocated needs, with the reverse situation existing in other cases. Then the problem is to achieve equality of supply and requirements. A commodity that appears to be in short supply may have its production plan increased. Alternatively the allocations of this deficit commodity to different users may be reduced. Efforts may be made to substitute more abundant for less abundant commodities. But, of course, any change in one balance affects other balances. A decision to increase the production of synthetic rubber, for example, means that the allocation of the chemicals required for rubber making must be raised. In turn, that change must be reflected in the balances for those chemicals. But to increase the production of these chemicals requires provision of larger amounts of the raw materials from which they are made, and this in its turn affects still other balances. A further complication is the fact that these changes cannot be made without serious constraints. For each user it is most important that there be consistency in all his assigned inputs. To revert to our tractor example, it is important that the industry receive all of the materials needed to produce 10,000 tractors—no more and no less. If more of one material is allocated than needed, that represents a waste and may mean that some other industry requiring more of this material than it has been allocated will suffer. On the other hand, if the tractor industry receives less of some important materials or components than it needs to produce 10,000 tractors, then its output of tractors will be limited to the number possible to produce with the scarcest material or component.

Soviet planners have traditionally tried to solve these problems of the method of balances by trial and error procedures. Given the immense magnitude of their task, it is dubious that they have ever gotten a completely integrated and completely consistent set of balances. Mistakes in the planning process have often had to be rectified at the grassroots, sometimes by the informal procedures described in the preceding chapter. In any case, *Gosplan's* chief concern has always been with the most important user agencies and industries and with the most critical materials and intermediate fabricated products, rather than with a mathematically satisfying system of equations.

Since the mid-1950's the use of electronic computers and the relaxation of ideological barriers have permitted *Gosplan* to make extensive experiments with input-output analysis, a technique of planning developed by Professor Wassily Leontief of Harvard University. In this analysis, a model of the relationships among the different industries of a given economy is set up by means of a series of linear equations. Essentially these equations link the gross outputs of different intermediate industries (steel, chemicals, electricity, etc.) with the final demands of an economy (consumer needs, defense requirements, net exports, etc.) In Western practice, it is customary to specify the final demands and solve for the needed gross outputs of intermediate industries. But the Soviet method of planning is based on the idea of specifying gross outputs, i.e., stating production targets for steel, electricity, and similar intermediate goods. Therefore what Soviet planners can do is to employ an input-output system of equations to solve for the final demands that can be satisfied with a planned set of gross outputs. They can experiment with different sets of gross outputs and compare the resulting sets of final demands gotten by solving the system of equations corresponding to each particular set of gross outputs. Moreover, by using an input-output system of equations, Soviet planners can calculate total input norms which provide important supplements to the direct input norms mentioned in our discussion of the method of balances. To revert to our tractor example again, we assumed that each tractor required two tons of steel as the direct input norm. But this ignored the steel required indirectly for tractor production, for example to build the tractor factory itself, to produce machinery used in the copper mine to turn out the required copper for tractors, and so on. The total input norms take account of both the direct and indirect materials requirements for tractor production and thus provide a fuller and more adequate accounting of the total costs of tractor production than do the direct input norms alone. [3]

Soviet economists clearly hope to improve the quality of their planning by extensive use of input-output analysis. An American

[3] Herbert S. Levine, "Input-Output Analysis and Soviet Planning," *American Economic Review*, May 1962, pp. 127-37. Oskar Lange, "Some Observations on Input-Output Analysis," in V. S. Nemchinov, *The Use of Mathematics in Economics* (Cambridge: The M.I.T. Press, 1964), p. 201.

specialist noted in late 1966 that "in the USSR alone, to date a total of 10 national input-output tables have been completed or are in preparation, ranging from the 83-industry table in value terms for 1959 to a mammoth 600 product table in physical units being prepared for 1970, the terminal year of the current 5-year plan. Some 20 regional or interregional tables have also been prepared."[4]

The decision to try to apply modern systems analysis and econometric techniques—input-output analysis, linear and other types of programming,—inevitably requires the widespread availability of powerful computers to perform the vast number of calculations involved. Toward this end, a decree of the Communist party Central Committee and the Council of Ministers announced in *Izvestia* on March 20, 1966, ordered the creation of a national system of government computer centers to gather and process economic information and to help solve the problems of economic planning and administration. The establishment of separate computer centers for different branches and departments of the Soviet Government was also ordered. The decree also provided for the institution of a special national organization to plan, install, and inaugurate a system using computers in economic management. The difficulties involved were suggested a month later, April 26, 1966, when *Izvestia* published an article by an official pointing out that not only were there technical difficulties—such as the lack of magnetic tape and the poor quality of Soviet punch cards—but also there were problems "in the preparation of the economic processes themselves for transfer to automatic machine processing. This work is exceptionally laborious and requires, as a rule, the significant revision of the most complex forms of planning and management, and also changes in the existing system of documentation."

Whatever help input-output analysis may give Soviet planners, it cannot eradicate a central weakness of the method of balances. This is the absence of any mechanism for optimizing the economic plan, for getting the greatest output from any given quantity of resource inputs, or for minimizing the volume of resource inputs required to produce a desired volume of output. Both the method of balances and that of input-output analysis take the existing structure and technology of production for granted. They do not inquire into such questions as whether aluminum should replace copper in tractor production or whether the fuel needs of the

---

[4]Vladimir G. Treml, "The 1959 Soviet Input-Output Table (As Reconstructed)," in *New Directions in the Soviet Economy*, Part II-A, p. 259.

country are best met by the existing mix of fuels or would be more economically met by reducing the output of some fuels and expanding the output of others. It is true that in trying to make their balances, Soviet economists will discover that some materials are in relatively shorter supply than others and they will try to make substitutions accordingly. But at best this is a crude procedure. The truth is that in the method of balances numerous decisions are made quite arbitrarily, and even when decisions are based upon comparisons of costs and prices they are not necessarily optimum decisions. This is because the Soviet price system does not reflect the relative scarcity of different commodities.

In the late 1930's, a Soviet mathematician, Leonid Kantorovich, invented linear programming, a technique for helping the planners to optimize their decisions. In a typical application of this technique, the conditions of an economic situation will be represented by a series of linear equations and inequalities. The key mathematical expression involved is the so-called objective function. This may represent the quantity to be maximized—perhaps profit or physical output—or the quantity to be minimized—perhaps cost per unit—in the given situation. Other equations and inequalities in a given problem will represent the constraints, born of limitations of resources, within which the objective function must be maximized or minimized as the case may be. Simple examples of this sort can be solved graphically, but more complex ones require electronic computers. A typical application might be to plan the most profitable schedule for an airline that has a fixed number of planes it must allocate to routes among cities each of which is characterized by a particular pattern of traffic. If Soviet planners wished they could also use Kantorovich's technique to obtain what are in effect rational prices to guide Soviet economic decisions. These shadow prices are called "objectively determined evaluators" by Kantorovich, and they measure the value of a scarce input in terms of what was sacrificed by not using that resource elsewhere in the economy. In technical terms, the objectively determined evaluators measure value in terms of opportunity cost.

In the Stalin era there was little high level Soviet interest in optimal planning. During the years immediately after World War II, in fact, mathematical economics was actively discouraged as an anti-Marxist heresy. Since Stalin's death, however, all this has changed. The Soviet Union has become a major center of research in econometrics and mathematical economics. Large resources are now devoted to the search for means of bringing Soviet planning closer to optimal allocation of resources. Soviet economists work intensively on mathematical models of economic activity, and explore energetically the application of input-output analysis and linear programming.[5]

A conference of Soviet mathematical economists, reported in the April 18, 1968 *Izvestia*, summed up both the accomplishments and problems of the efforts made until then to optimize Soviet economic planning. Already in the 1966-1970 Five Year Plan, the scheduled growth of the Soviet cement industry had been dictated by an economic plan based on mathematical methods of optimization. For the Ninth Five Year Plan, covering 1971-1975, the intention was stated of optimizing 74 branch economic plans, 12 of these dealing with the production of various building materials. Academician N. Fedorenko told the conference that optimization of the structure of plastics production during 1971-1975 would alone give the Soviet Union a gain of one billion rubles. Another speaker asserted that the advantages of applying mathematical methods in economic planning had no less significance for the Soviet economy than application of the techniques of atomic physics.

The speakers at the conference also underlined the many difficulties facing them. They noted there were no adequate arrangements for financing such econometric planning; they deplored the extreme shortage of personnel trained in mathematical economics; and they complained much about the extreme inadequacy of the number of computers available to do the needed computations. But the chief problem indicated at the conference was the widespread bureaucratic resistance to introduction of optimization techniques, resistance coming from planning officials who either know little about econometrics or who have no personal financial interest in aiding the adoption of improved plans. Perhaps most fundamental, however, was the objection of economist V. Dmitriev who noted that many wholesale prices are still far from their optimal levels and who then asked, in *Izvestia*'s words, "How can mathematical calculations be built on such prices?"

---

[5] For further information see Heinz Köhler, *Welfare and Planning* (New York: John Wiley & Sons, Inc., 1966), Alfred Zauberman, *Aspects of Planometrics* (New Haven: Yale University Press, 1967), and John P. Hardt, Marvin Hoffenberg, Norman Kaplan and Herbert S. Levine, eds., *Mathematics and Computers in Soviet Economic Planning* (New Haven: Yale University Press, 1967).

## The Soviet Price System

We will consider now the Soviet price system, the key to any comprehensive effort to optimize the operation of the nation's economy. The four major components of this system are the following: free market prices for foods, state retail prices for consumer goods and foods, industrial wholesale prices, and agricultural procurement prices. Of these four only the free market prices are formed spontaneously under the influence of supply and demand; the others are set by the state on many different bases. Retail prices are set with some eye to equalizing supply and demand, although often they are too low—producing shortages and black markets—and sometimes they are too high—producing large inventories of unsold goods. Soviet retail prices bear no fixed relation to costs of production. Many consumer goods are priced far above their costs, the difference being reflected in large turnover taxes—sales taxes in effect—collected by the state. On the other hand, in recent years the retail prices of meat have produced losses for the state, while the retail prices of milk, milk products, and fish have been near the point of producing losses. [6]

During the Stalin era, agricultural procurement prices for most products were set at very low levels so as to squeeze capital from the farm sector. The increases since 1953 have been motivated by the need to provide incentives for an adequate volume of production. In making farm price changes this past decade, some attention has been paid to the results of studies of costs of production of agricultural output and also to studies of regional variations of these costs. [7] The failure of the farm price increases under Khrushchev to provide an adequate volume of output in the early 1960's induced his successors to announce additional price rises in 1965.

Our chief interest here is the industrial wholesale price system. These wholesale prices define the terms on which Soviet enterprises buy and sell goods from one another. In the main, these prices have been based on planned average costs of production for a given commodity at the different major plants producing it, plus a small profit, usually 5 per cent of cost. In these calculations, before 1966, there was no allowance for interest on capital, or for

---

[6] V. Sitnin, "Khozyaistvennaya Reforma i Peresmotr Optovykh Tsen na Promyshlennuyu Produktsiyu," *Kommunist*, No. 14, 1966, p. 40.

[7] Morris Bornstein, "The Soviet Price System," *American Economic Review*, March 1962, pp. 64-103.

rent on land and other scarce natural resources used in production. Traditionally, depreciation allowances included in Soviet costs and prices have been notoriously inadequate. For these reasons alone, Soviet prices have often failed to reflect actual costs and have distorted cost comparisons between different commodities, for example between commodities requiring much capital and others requiring little capital in their production.

From the point of view of constructing a rational price system that will reflect relative scarcities, this emphasis on costs as bases for prices is grossly deficient because it ignores the factor of demand. Moreover, even if it were granted that a particular Soviet wholesale price structure was acceptable at the time it was created, it would clearly become more and more unacceptable with the passage of time and the accompanying changes in costs and demands. Most industrial wholesale prices introduced by Soviet authorities in 1955 were maintained until 1967, despite the fact that this was a period of rapid technological and other change—in many branches of production.

Basing its view on Marx's labor theory of value, orthodox Soviet economic theory has held that prices must reflect socially necessary labor costs. But by 1966 it was clear that the 1955 price system did not do that. Important raw materials such as coal, iron and manganese ores, and sulphuric acid were priced so low that the producing industries did not receive compensation for their costs of production even by the Soviet definition of costs. These industries had to be subsidized by the state. In turn, metals and other products of later stages of fabrication were underpriced since their quotations were based in part on the inadequate raw material prices. Moreover, in general the 1955 prices made grossly inadequate allowances for quality differences among different grades of the same commodity. Hence it was frequently unprofitable for a factory to incur the additional costs required to produce higher quality goods even though it would have been profitable for its customers to buy the superior goods and to obtain the economies they would have made possible. Finally, by 1964, the existing industrial wholesale price system had produced a chaotic profit situation. The coal industry that year had a loss equivalent to 16 per cent of its capital, while the instrument manufacturing industry had annual profits equal to 50 per cent of its capital. The situation was even more complex within particular industries: "In any industry there are many examples where the production of some items is unprofitable, while others provide profits of 200-300 or more per cent." The Soviet official who pointed this out argued that as a result existing prices were unsuitable guides for enterprise directors working under the economic reform with its pressure for maximizing profits. He feared that such profit diversity would lead to neglect of the output of essential goods that brought little or no profit.[8]

The new industrial wholesale prices introduced on July 1, 1967, take into some account the cost of capital. Prices are based on average costs, as before, plus a profit allowance usually calculated as 15 per cent of an industry's capital investment. If demand was taken into account, it was usually done indirectly, as in the new emphasis on providing price differentials for goods of varying quality as well as in the effort made to link prices of mutually substitutable goods, for example, coal, oil and gas. Among the key price increases introduced were rises of 78 per cent for coal, 130 per cent for iron ore, 80 per cent for oil sold to oil refineries, 51 per cent for gas, 43 per cent for rolled ferrous metals, 22 per cent for non-ferrous metals, and 13 per cent for cement.[9] The large increases in coal and metal ore prices were intended to make profits possible in these hitherto deficit-ridden industries, but even the 78 per cent rise in the coal price was reckoned to make possible only little more than a 7.5 per cent rate of profit on that industry's capital. The iron and steel industry's profit rate on capital was raised from 8 to 15 per cent, but the chemical industry's corresponding profit rate was lowered from 20 to 15 per cent. In setting machinery prices, the rate of return on capital was set at somewhat less than 15 per cent, in part because of the desire to keep down prices on machines sold to farmers. For heavy industry as a whole, the reform required an average price rise of 11-12 per cent. In consumer goods industry, prices were set at levels producing annual rates of return of 30-35 per cent on capital investment. Taking into account the different production costs for oil and gas obtained under different natural conditions, prices were set on the basis of costs under worse than average conditions; enterprises working under more favorable conditions were required to make "rent payments" to the Soviet treasury.[10]

---

[8] Sitnin, *op. cit.*, p. 38.

[9] A. Komin, "Peresmotr Optovykh Tsen i Priblizheniye ix k Obshchestvenno Neobkhodimym Zatratam," *Voprosy Ekonomiki*, No. 4, 1967, P. 26.

[10] Sitnin, *op. cit.*, pp. 40-43, and A. Komin, "Problemy Sovershenstvovaniya Tsen Promyshlennosti," *Planovoye Khozyaistvo*, October 1966, pp. 10-16. For a more detailed discussion cf. *Ekonomicheskaya Gazeta*, No. 27, July 1967, p. 10.

The price reform undoubtedly represents some progress. But it is unlikely that the new 1967 prices adequately reflect relative scarcity. Presumably, further improvements will be made in the future on the basis of the work of the important and increasingly influential Soviet mathematical economists. Such leading figures as V.V. Novozhilov and L.V. Kantorovich have taught their colleagues and superiors that optimum use of resources requires value calculations based on prices that take into account the scarcities of resources relative to demand. Professor Kantorovich's linear programming techniques, as noted above, provide a means of calculating so-called "shadow prices" that take these scarcities into account. In different writings, Kantorovich has called these "shadow prices" by such terms as "objectively determined evaluators" and "resolving multipliers." Novozhilov has tackled the problem of fulfilling a plan consisting of specified production targets at minimum cost in terms of labor expenditure. His results indicate the need to take into account certain "indirect labor costs" which arise from using scarce natural resources and capital for one purpose rather than another. In Western terminology, these are the opportunity costs of using scarce resources. The result is that Novozhilov's "indirect labor costs" are analogous to interest on capital and rent on natural resources. Of course, neither Kantorovich nor Novozhilov nor their colleagues envisage the payment of interest to private Soviet capitalists or the payment of rent to private Soviet landlords. But such payments to private persons are not required to make use of these concepts as tools which help take explicit account of the scarcity of capital and of natural resources in making allocations. In effect, these men and their colleagues have rediscovered much of Western micro-economic value theory, have worked out ingenious rationalizations to make that theory acceptable to Marxists, and have pressed for increasing use of this theory in solving the practical problems of Soviet economics. Much still remains to be done, however. [11]

Authoritative Soviet spokesmen indicated repeatedly in 1968 their intention to make Soviet prices more flexible and more responsive to change in the future. Writing in *Voprosy Ekonomiki,*

[11] There are important articles by Kantorovich and Novozhilov in Nemchinov, *op. cit.* Kantorovich's major work is *The Best Use of Economic Resources* (Cambridge: Harvard University Press, 1965). See also Robert W. Campbell, "Marx Kantorovich and Novozhilov," *Slavic Review,* October 1961, pp. 402-18, and Howard J. Sherman, "Marxist Economics and Soviet Planning," *Soviet Studies,* October 1966, pp. 169-88.

No. 5, 1968, for example, the Chairman of the State Prices Committee, V. Sitnin, spoke of annual price reviews for different types of machinery, chemicals, and building materials. One purpose of these reviews will be to cut prices of old products so as to make them less profitable and thus stimulate a search for new goods, new processes, and new designs. To facilitate these more frequent price changes, the Soviet regime created a Special Fund for Wholesale Price Regulation at the beginning of 1968. Under the control of the State Prices Committee, this fund will be used to compensate producers when prices are lowered and purchasers when prices are increased so as to ease the initial impact of price changes on those adversely affected. A description of this fund and its operation was given in *Ekonomicheskaya Gazeta*, No. 19, May 1968.

Some of the most serious errors resulting from the irrational Soviet price system are found in the field of capital investment. The absence of an explicit interest rate has caused Soviet planners systematically to underestimate the real costs of capital investment projects and of the output they provide. The Soviet fondness for hydroelectric power plants is a prime example. These projects and others like them tied up scarce capital for long periods before giving any output. The substantial costs incurred thereby were not taken into account. Nikita Khrushchev recognized the problem in the summer of 1958 when he complained about the building of large hydroelectric stations. He argued then:

> We built the 2,300,000 kilowatt Lenin Volga Hydroelectric
> Station in seven years . . . But with the same money we could
> have built in less time several thermal power plants with a to
> tal capacity of 11,000,000 kilowatts. True, the electric power
> from thermal plants is more expensive, but on the other hand
> they will supply power to our factories much earlier . . . [12]

Khrushchev was really complaining against the Soviet planners' practice of deciding among capital investment alternatives for a given purpose by picking the one which minimized annual operating costs. Thus, given a choice between generating electricity by burning coal (whose cost was included in these calculations) or by building a dam (interest on whose cost of construction was not counted), Soviet planners tended to regard it as self-evident that the hydroelectric power was cheaper. For a time in the mid-1950's they showed similar mistaken favoritism to atomic power

[12] *Pravda*, August 24, 1958.

plants. In transportation, problems of this sort arose. Should a railroad line connecting two cities be built over the shortest distance if this meant heavy capital investment in building bridges over intervening rivers and boring tunnels through intervening mountains? Or should it be built over a more circuitous route that would avoid most of these investments, but would require more fuel expenditure per trip?

In the late 1950's, Soviet economists won official approval for use of a systematic technique to make judgments about alternative capital investments. The basic problem they sought to solve can be stated in this way. There exist two (or more, but the same principles apply) ways of performing a given task. One involves a capital investment outlay $C_1$ and an annual operating cost (wages, raw materials, depreciation, etc.) $E_1$ while the other involves similarly an investment outlay of $C_2$ and a corresponding annual operating cost of $E_2$. Which should be chosen? Clearly, if one project had both the lower capital outlay and the lower annual operating cost, it was the superior choice; then no real problem existed. But how should the choice be made if, say, the first alternative's capital cost was greater but its annual operating cost lower, i.e., $C_1 > C_2$ and $E_1 < E_2$? In this case, Soviet planners were urged to use either the Coefficient of Relative Effectiveness or its reciprocal, the recoupment period. The Coefficient of Relative Effectiveness (C.R.E.) was defined as the difference in annual operating costs divided by the difference in capital outlays, that is:

$$\frac{E_2 - E_1}{C_1 - C_2}.$$

A coefficient of 20 per cent would mean that by using the more capital intensive variant, one would have an economy in annual operating costs amounting to 20 per cent of the extra investment. A C.R.E. of 20 per cent would be equivalent to a recoupment period of five years. This means that if the more capital intensive project were used, its extra capital investment would be regained in five years from the annual savings in current operating costs. Using either of these two measures, then, a decision could be made by comparing the C.R.E. or the recoupment period for a given set of alternatives with an approved general norm. Thus in the numerical example cited, the capital intensive variant would be chosen if the acceptable norm were a C.R.E. of 10 per cent, or its equivalent, a recoupment period of ten years. On the other hand, the less capital intensive project would be chosen in our example if the norm were a C.R.E. of 25 per cent, or a recoupment period of four years. In actual Soviet practice, different norms are used in different industries, presumably leading to quite different choices between more and less intensive capital investment opportunities in different fields. [13]

The use of this device to aid rational choice is certainly better than ignoring the capital investment factor altogether. But its utility is weakened by the fact that the prices in which both capital investment and current operating costs are stated are not prices reflecting relative scarcity. Moreover, a prominent Soviet economist has complained publicly that "in the planning of capital construction, the methods economists have worked out to measure the effectiveness of capital investment are almost not taken into account." [14]

This economist, academician Khachaturov, has stressed the importance of maximizing the effectiveness of capital investment to reverse the downward trend in the production return per unit of capital investment. In the Seven Year Plan period, 1959-1965, he has estimated, this return declined 17 per cent, and if the Eighth Five Year Plan for 1966-1970 is fulfilled, that return will decline another 6.5 per cent. Among the causes he notes are such factors as the increasing volume of investment in Siberia where costs are above average, and the need to utilize poorer natural resources. However, he also stresses the detrimental effect of poor capital investment planning, complaining: "It is impossible further to reconcile oneself to situations where first the question of necessity of building one or another installation is decided, and then the search begins for an economic justification." [15]

---

[13] Abram Bergson, *The Economics of Soviet Planning* (New Haven: Yale University Press, 1964), pp. 253-61.

[14] T. S. Khachaturov in *Pravda*, March 15, 1966.

[15] T.S. Khachaturov, "Ekonomicheskaya Effectivnost Kapitalnykh Vlozheni," *Kommunist*, No. 13, September 1966, p. 69.

# Financial Aspects of the Soviet Economy 5

It has been many decades since Soviet leaders or economists spoke seriously of abolishing money. Today money is employed in the Soviet economy for many of the same purposes as in non-Communist lands. Soviet workers and farmers are paid 'in cash which they then use to buy goods and services as well as to pay state taxes. Transactions among Soviet enterprises are conducted in monetary terms. Private Soviet citizens can deposit money in savings banks, which pay 2 per cent interest. Money can be bequeathed and inherited. Much of the coordination of the Soviet economy is accomplished through plans expressed in monetary terms, plans designed to be the financial counterparts of the production plans stated in physical units of different commodities. And, of course, the 1965 economic reform's emphasis on the importance of enterprise sales and profits further raised the importance of monetary factors in Soviet life. Against this background, we shall examine the Soviet monetary system and Soviet financial planning with emphasis on the budget as well as the Soviet banking complex.

## Soviet Money

Repeated unhappy experience with inflation in the first years of Soviet rule, in the 1930's, and during and immediately after World War II has made the Soviet authorities fiscal and monetary conservatives.[1] They place high value on keeping the purchasing power of their currency stable or increasing; they believe in balanced budgets and they eschew the manipulation of monetary policy so prevalent in the West. Occasionally they voice hopes of making the ruble so strong that it can become an international currency, competing with and perhaps displacing the American dollar and the British pound. But the realization of this ambition seems distant. Soviet currency is still entirely a domestic economic instrument whose export and import—except in very limited amounts—is prohibited.

The present monetary system of the Soviet Union—based on a ruble worth 100 kopeks—derives essentially from the monetary reform of December 1947. The aim of that reform was to wipe out the inflationary heritage of World War II by, in effect, confiscating most of the large currency hoards accumulated by those who had been able to sell food and other goods at high prices during and after the war. This was done by issuing new rubles that were exchanged for existing money at different rates. These rates ranged from ten old rubles for one new ruble in the case of cash, to one old ruble for one new ruble for private bank accounts under 3,000 rubles. The move was a major devaluation since prices, taxes, and wages were maintained unchanged. This major reduction in the amount of purchasing power available to the Soviet public facilitated the accompanying transition from a rationing system to normal state retail trade. Another major change came on February 28, 1950, when the ruble was defined in terms of gold rather than of the American dollar, as formerly. The gold content of the ruble was declared to be equal to .222168 grams of pure gold, though no provision was made for permitting Soviet citizens to buy gold at this price with their rubles or for foreign monetary authorities to exchange rubles for gold. Simultaneously, the ruble was unilaterally revalued in terms of the dollar; four rubles were declared equal to one dollar as against 5.3 rubles to the dollar earlier. Both the old and the new exchange rates grossly exaggerated the real value of the

---

[1] For the early history of Soviet money see Schwartz, *Russia's Soviet Economy*, pp. 470-78.

ruble, a fact implicitly admitted later in the 1950's when Western tourists were permitted to buy ten rubles for each dollar.

At the beginning of 1961, a new "heavy ruble" was introduced. This was done by exchanging all Soviet currency (and also proportionately changing all Soviet prices, taxes, and obligations) for a new currency at the rate of ten old rubles for one new ruble. Simultaneously the ruble was devalued in terms of the dollar. The new "heavy ruble" was declared equal to $1.11, rather than to the $2.50 it would have been set equal to had the 10:1 conversion ratio been applied here too. The effect of this devaluation was to make the official Soviet ruble-dollar exchange rate more realistic than earlier. Also, this move permitted abolition of the favorable special tourist ruble-dollar exchange rate. In the early 1960's, too, a "transferable ruble" was introduced as the accounting unit for the Soviet Bloc's new International Bank for Economic Cooperation, but this transferable unit is not a currency and has no real relationship with the separate Soviet internal ruble system.

## Soviet Financial Planning

Soviet financial planning, which is the responsibility of the State Planning Committee, the Ministry of Finance, and the State Bank, seeks to assure that the flow of funds through the economy aids the fulfillment of the overall economic plan. These funds are of two kinds, and the circuits they make are to a large extent independent. There is cash, the medium of exchange between the state and the population, and also among members of the population; and there is credit, almost all of which is extended by the State Bank to state enterprises and organizations. Payments among enterprises which buy from and sell to each other may not be made in cash above a small maximum amount. Instead, a giant bookkeeping apparatus maintained by the State Bank debits and credits the appropriate bank accounts. There are some forms of consumer credit—for example, limited time payment plans to finance some consumer purchases and loans to finance home building—but their aggregate volume is relatively small, and they play no role approaching that of consumer credit in the West.

Four key plans dominate Soviet financial planning: the *state budget*, an integrated document covering all levels—national, provincial, and local—of Soviet Government income and expenditure, and accounting for the disposition in recent years of amounts exceeding half the Soviet national income; the *cash plan* and the *credit plan,* the latter divided into short and long term credit parts; and the *plan for the balance of the population's money income and expenditures.* The purpose of the latter plan is to try to assure essential equality between the money the citizens will have available to spend and the value of goods and services available for purchase plus taxes and voluntary savings. The goal is to try to avoid significant inflationary pressures.[2] All these plans are, in theory at least, integrated with the economic plans stated in physical units so that the study of the fulfillment of the financial plans is to a large extent also study of the fulfillment of the overall commodity production and distribution plans.

The nature of the Soviet budget, which covers all governmental units, is best illustrated by Table 7 which shows Soviet budget revenues and expenditures for several recent years.

On the revenue side of the Soviet budget, the most striking trend has been the declining share of the turnover tax and the increasing importance of income from profits of state enterprises. The turnover tax is essentially a general sales tax with varying but often very heavy rates on consumer goods and food. This tax accounted for almost two-thirds of all Soviet state revenue in 1938 and over half in 1950. By 1968 turnover tax receipts had grown sharply but they provided only about one-third of budgetary revenue. Turnover tax income since 1952 has not kept pace with rising food and consumer goods output because the Soviet state has several times increased the prices paid farmers. Except for the time the Soviet regime raised retail meat and butter prices sharply in 1962, it has usually not increased prices to consumers to compensate for the higher prices paid farmers since Stalin's death. The resulting decline in the Soviet government's profit margin has been absorbed by a decline in the corresponding rates of turnover tax. In the 1960's much or most of the turnover tax revenue has come from sales of tobacco products, vodka or other alcoholic beverages, textiles, clothing, sugar and consumer durable goods. But more than compensating for the slow growth of total turnover tax revenues has been the rapid increase in the contribution to the state's income provided by enterprise

---

[2] See the detailed forms of these plans in George Garvy, *Money, Banking and Credit in Eastern Europe* (New York: Federal Reserve Bank of New York, 1966), pp. 53-64. Cf. also his "The Role of the State Bank in Soviet Planning," in Jane Degras, ed., *Soviet Planning Essays in Honor of Naum Jasny* (New York: Frederick A. Praeger, Inc.. 1964), pp. 46-76.

profits. This rising contribution has reflected both the speedy increase in Soviet industrial production and success in lowering costs. In the current economic reform, the flow of enterprise profits into the state budget is being restructured. Instead of arbitrarily fixing certain percentages of enterprise profits to be paid the state, the government plans more and more to tap prof-

**TABLE 7.**  The Soviet Budget, 1960-1968

| | 1960 | 1964 | 1967° | 1968 (plan) |
|---|---|---|---|---|
| | | (billion rubles) | | |
| Revenues | 77.1 | 94.4 | 115.5 | 123.8 |
| Turnover tax | 31.3 | 36.7 | 40.9 | 42.2 |
| Deductions from profits, interest on capital, and related payments | 18.6 | 28.7 | 39.6 | 43.8 |
| Income taxes from cooperatives, collective farms, and other non-state enterprises | 1.8 | 1.3 | † | † |
| State loans | .9 | .1 | † | † |
| Direct taxes on population | 5.6 | 6.8 | 9.2 | 10.3 |
| Social insurance payments | 3.8 | 5.0 | 6.6 | † |
| Expenditures | 73.1 | 92.2 | 114.5 | 123.5 |
| National economy | 34.1 | 40.6 | 49.9 | 50.1 |
| Defense | 9.3 | 13.3 | 14.5 | 16.7 |
| Education, science, culture | 10.3 | 15.1 | 19.9 | 21.0 |
| Health and physical culture | 4.8 | 5.6 | 7.4 | 7.6 |
| Social security | 6.5 | 8.6 | 16.1 | 17.1 |
| Social insurance | 2.8 | 3.5 | 16.1 | 17.1 |
| Administration | 1.1 | 1.1 | 1.5 | 1.5 |

° Expected fulfillment.
† Not available.
Sources: *Narkhoz 1964*, p. 770. *Pravda*, December 8, 1965, and October 11, 1967. *SSSR v Tsifrakh v 1967 godu*, p. 29.

its by requiring payments covering the interest on enterprise capital (6 per cent initially) and "rent" charges for exploitation of oil and other mineral resources having differential advantages as regards location, quality, ease of recovery or the like.

Another recent major change in Soviet revenues was the revision of the income tax levied on Soviet collective farms. Before January 1, 1966, the tax was a standard 12.5 per cent on each *kolkhoz's* gross income in cash and produce, less an allowance for money and produce used in production. The new tax has been levied in two parts: one is a 12 per cent tax on each *kolkhoz's* net income in excess of a 15 per cent profit on its total costs; the other is an 8 per cent tax on that portion of the *kolkhoz* wage fund in excess of 60 rubles a month for each *kolkhoz* worker. In presenting the Soviet budget for 1966, the Soviet Minister of Finance indicated that collective farms would have paid almost 1.2 billion rubles under the old system but would actually pay only 700,000,000 rubles under the new arrangement.[3]

The personal income tax in the Soviet Union has never been a major source of revenue. Its highest rate for government employees is 13 per cent on wages over 100 rubles a month. The preference for hidden turnover taxation over personal income taxes as an important source of state revenue is apparently born of political and administrative factors. The personal income tax is much more visible and tends to produce more resentment than the turnover tax whose existence is rarely called to the attention of those who pay it. Soviet authorities, who seek to make their wage and salary system a means of providing incentives, thus look with disfavor on a high progressive income tax. In this respect, they agree with many conservative opponents of the United States income tax. Ideally, Soviet authorities would prefer to have no personal income tax at all. In 1960 a five year program unveiled by Khrushchev provided for the abolition of the Soviet income tax in stages, but in 1962 Soviet financial difficulties forced a halt in this program and its indefinite postponement. The two stages of income tax reduction that were carried out in the early 1960's benefited primarily the lowest paid groups of Soviet workers. In 1968 a further step provided an average 25 per cent cut in the income tax on earnings of 61-80 rubles a month.[4]

---

[3] *Selskaya Zhizn*, April 24, 1965, and *Pravda*, December 8, 1965.

[4] Schwartz, *The Soviet Economy Since Stalin*, pp. 176-78, and *Pravda*, October 11, 1967.

On the expenditure side of the Soviet budget, we note that the largest single component consists of sums used to finance the national economy. In this category the Soviet regime provides fixed capital and part of the working capital for its enterprises, thus implementing the investment decisions contained in the annual economic plan. This section of the budget finances government housing construction, the building of new factories, dams, rail lines and the like. It also provides subsidies to plants and industries which have "planned losses." Of the 50.1 billion rubles included in this category in the planned 1968 budget, 23.9 billion rubles were to go to industry, 9.0 billion rubles to agriculture, and 5.9 billion rubles to housing construction. [5]

The defense appropriation included in the Soviet budget is a major enigma since the total amount is published without any supporting detail. The suspicion is strong among Western analysts that much spending on military preparation is hidden in other categories; for example, military research is almost certainly included in the overall scientific research appropriation, or not mentioned at all. A Soviet source reports that the budget of the Ministry of Defense includes the following items:

(1) Payments for supplies to the army, air force and navy of armaments, ammunition and technical equipment, fuel and lubricants, and foodstuffs, clothing and other items needed for state military preparedness;
(2) financing the capital construction and industrial enterprises of the Ministry of Defense of the U.S.S.R.;
(3) other requirements for the military and political training and the administration and welfare provision of military units;
(4) provision of pay for servicemen in the Soviet Army. [6]

Unfortunately, however, no corresponding numerical breakdown of the global Soviet defense budget is published.

The "welfare state" aspects of the Soviet system are financed through budgetary appropriations covering education, public health, social security, and social insurance. These funds pay for the entire school system from kindergarten to graduate school, for the entire medical system, for old-age pensions, sick pay, disability pensions, and similar benefits. Costs of these services are very substantial and they have increased rapidly in recent years, especially after significant wage increases were given in 1964 and 1965 to many categories of workers in these areas. So-

---

[5] *Pravda, op. cit.*

[6] *Soviet Financial System* (Moscow: Progress Publishers, 1966), p. 269.

viet pensions have also been made more adequate in recent years.

The increasing costs of the Soviet welfare programs are burdensome to the Soviet government and much thought has been given to shifting some of these costs to consumers of social services. In December 1966 it was revealed that special clinics have been set up at which patients must pay for consultations but can choose their doctors. This was revealed in the course of a plea for the establishment of nursing homes and hospitals at which patients would pay, a plea justified by admission that free Soviet hospitals are so overcrowded that their patients have to be sent home before they are really well.[7] On a related matter there have been hints from time to time of behind the scenes debates about raising rents on housing. These have traditionally been so low that they do not even pay for adequate maintenance of existing housing, let alone cover depreciation and provide funds for additional housing construction. The encouragement given to the construction of cooperative apartment houses—whose future occupants pay construction costs—is indicative of the interest in cutting down the costs of social welfare measures.

Even in this summary discussion mention must be made of the rising Soviet budgetary expenditures on scientific research. In 1950 such research was assigned 539 million rubles; by 1960 the allotment reached slightly over four billion rubles; and the 1968 budget allowed 7.9 billion rubles for this purpose. The latter amount, it may be noted, exceeded the total appropriation for the entire system of socialized medicine that year. Presumably, most of this scientific research is on rockets, nuclear weapons and other needs of the Soviet military and space research efforts.

## The Soviet Banking System

As of mid-1968, the Soviet Union had three banks: the State Bank (*Gosbank*), the Construction Bank (*Stroibank*), and the Bank for Foreign Trade (*Vneshtorgbank*).[8] The Construction Bank has been primarily concerned with the distribution of government appropriations for capital investment to specific enterprises and

---

[7] *New York Times*, December 9, 1966, p. 7.

[8] For historical background on the Soviet banking system, cf. Schwartz, *Russia's Soviet Economy*, pp. 505-15, and Gregory Grossman, "Gold and Sword: Money in the Soviet Command Economy," in Henry Rosovsky, ed., *Industrialization in Two Systems: Essays in Honor of Alexander Gerschenkron* (New York: John Wiley & Sons, Inc., 1966), pp. 204-36.

with overseeing the utilization of these funds. The Bank for Foreign Trade is assigned the task of financing much of the Soviet Union's foreign trade. We shall focus here on the State Bank, a giant organization which performs the great bulk of all Soviet banking and related operations.

The State Bank issues Soviet currency and is charged with regulating the nation's currency supply, as well as with being the financial agent of the Soviet state. As of January 1, 1967, the State Bank had 164 regional offices, almost 4,000 local commercial branches, and 75,000 savings bank offices. Through its network of savings bank offices—joined to the State Bank in 1963—it collects the savings of millions of Soviet citizens and also provides facilities for the payment of taxes, rent, and public utility bills to state agencies. The primary function of the State Bank, however, is to exercise financial supervision over the economy—"control by the ruble" in Soviet jargon. It exercises this function by means of its roles as the central clearing agency for purchase and sale transactions between Soviet enterprises, as the distributor of cash which enterprises employ to pay their workers, and as the source of virtually all short-term credit for Soviet enterprises as well as of an increasing amount of longer term credits. Historically, the State Bank has regarded itself as a financial policeman, checking the activities of Soviet enterprises and institutions to make sure they conform to their plans. The Bank regulates its disbursements of credit and cash to enterprises not only in accord with the state's financial plans, but also in the light of how well or how poorly different enterprises are doing in fulfilling their production assignments and maintaining financial discipline.

The rapid growth of the Soviet economy has increased the number of financial transactions and has sharply raised the volume of credit extended. In 1951, for example, credit outstanding at the beginning of the year amounted to 17.3 billion rubles of short-term credit and 2.0 billion rubles of long-term credit. At the beginning of 1966 the figures were 68.0 billion rubles of short-term credit and 6.0 billion rubles of long-term credit outstanding. Similarly, the rising incomes of Soviet citizens—resulting from higher wages for workers and increased prices and incomes received by farmers—resulted in savings banks deposit accumulations rising over the same period from 1.8 to 18.7 billion rubles. Even at the beginning of 1967, though, the average size of a Soviet savings account was only 377 rubles. [9]

---

[9] *Narkhoz 1965*, p. 600 and *Strana Sovetov za 50 Let*, p. 254.

The credit extension activities of the State Bank consist mainly, as indicated above, of short-term credits intended to supplement the working capital of individual enterprises. Access to these credits is governed by a plant's needs as it seeks to fulfill its physical production and sales plans, and not by consideration of the profitability of each loan. Short-term credits help enterprises carry inventory, either at times of seasonal peaks of operation or at times of unexpected need, for example, when an interruption in the supply of some vital part delays shipment of finished items. Credit is also used to bridge the period between shipment of goods and receipt of payment, and to help restore an enterprise's working capital when it has been temporarily depleted. Of course, credit serves also as an instrument whose denial can be used to discourage excessive inventory accumulation. Historically Soviet bankers have sought to issue short-term credits to serve specific purposes and to have tangible collateral for each loan. But these requirements have weakened over time, for example, as credits have been allowed for wage payments (where there is no collateral) and as there has been increasing tendency to gear credits to the flow of output and the total turnover of an enterprise. The latter practice comes close to providing automatic credit to finance an agreed percentage of an enterprise's raw materials and other inventory.[10] Longer term loans, stretching over periods of several years, have been permitted since the mid-1950's to finance relatively small capital investments in modern machinery and to purchase equipment needed to produce consumer goods where such investments have not been included in the enterprise's basic financial plan.

The. economic reform of 1965 has encouraged new ideas for changes in the Soviet financial system. At the extreme, voices have argued, in effect, that planned distribution of credits be abandoned and that the Soviet banking system emulate the West. These radical thinkers have urged that Soviet bankers be permitted to put their credit resources up for auction and make loans to those enterprises prepared to pay the highest rates of interest. These reformers also suggest that bonuses be paid to Soviet bankers on the basis of how profitably they are able to· employ their loanable funds. Other radical reformers would have the banks give up their inspection and police functions. These critics argue that bank economists simply do not know enough

---

[10] Garvy, *op. cit.*, pp. 75-81.

about all the different types of production to propose very much that is really helpful to management and the state. These views in the financial field are the counterpart of the arguments elsewhere which recommended shifting the entire Soviet economy toward a free market organization, and eliminating or drastically limiting central planning.

The new banking regulations adopted by the Council of Ministers on April 3, 1967, embodied a series of changes very much in the spirit of the cautious and limited overall 1965 Soviet economic reform.[11] Under the new regulations, enterprises are required to get credits for 40 to 50 per cent of the value of the goods they buy and of other production costs. The enterprise working capital displaced by this compulsory use of credit is placed in a special account in the State Bank which has these funds available to extend credit as it sees fit. The justification has been offered that this forced greater reliance on credit will "stimulate fulfillment of sales plans as well as strict observance of contractual obligations regarding deliveries of goods and payment for them."

Most generally, the intent of these 1967 changes was to increase somewhat the independence and scope of action of branches of the State Bank, to give enterprises greater incentives for financial good behavior, to expand the purposes for which the State Bank can give longer term credits, and to increase the importance of a differentiated set of interest rates as an instrument of economic control. Thus the State Bank can now give emergency 30-day loans to finance wage payments by enterprises in temporary difficulties and 60-day loans to enterprises offering as security their excessive inventories of raw materials or other goods. Both the State Bank and the Construction Bank are permitted to issue loans for periods of up to six years to enterprises wishing to modernize their equipment or to improve the organization of their production mechanism. Local officials of these banks are permitted to authorize such loans for amounts up to 100,000 rubles, while provincial bank officials can approve such loans up to 300,000 rubles. Whereas State Bank short-term interest rates had been one or two per cent annually since the early 1930's, the new interest rate schedule for different types of loans ranges from 1 per cent for loans facilitating the clearing of purchase-sale transactions to 8 per cent for overdue loans.

---

[11] The text of the new regulations appeared in *Ekonomicheskaya Gazeta*, No. 17, April 1967, pp. 3-4. Cf. also No. 20, May 1967, pp. 9-10 for a valuable commentary.

Many types of loans bear interest rates equal to the government charge on an enterprise's capital, that is, 6 per cent. To increase enterprise independence, the State Bank is now forbidden to declare enterprises bankrupt or to put them under special payment regimens because of past deficiencies in paying their bills. Responsibility for taking special measures toward such bad credit risks is now put on the enterprises selling the goods. The seller may require various measures amounting to preliminary guarantee of payment before shipping the commodities that have been ordered.

All this seems mild enough to Westerners, but in the Soviet Union these and related changes occasioned serious debate. In fact, these changes in credit and payment regulations were not issued until a year and a half after the basic Soviet economic reform had been announced. Even with the reform, the conservatism and central plan orientation of the banking system continued. This was revealed by the new regulations for bonuses to banking system employees approved on April 18, 1967. These regulations make bonuses dependent upon results in insuring the rapid return of cash to the bank and in securing timely payment of loans. Skill in making loans and in otherwise allocating loanable funds goes unmentioned as a reason for earning bonuses.[12]

The above discussion has been primarily concerned with the banking system's relations with non-agricultural branches of the Soviet economy. But the increased priority given agriculture since Stalin's death and the greater flow of money through agriculture as government prices have been increased have also been reflected in increased relationships between the banking system and the farms, particularly collective farms. Long-term credits to collective farms increased five-fold between the beginning of 1951 and 1966, from 658 million rubles to 3.9 billion rubles; short-term farm production credits are also increasing. In view of this, the banking system has been experimenting in recent years with various means of establishing direct credit relations between the *kolkhozy* and local branches of the State Bank.

As of late 1967, two-thirds of all long-term loans extended by the State Bank to *kolkhozy* were either to purchase tractors and combines or to finance the building of barns and other productive structures. These loans carried an infinitesimal interest rate— three-quarters of 1 per cent annually—and were repayable over

---

[12] *Ekonomicheskaya Gazeta*, No. 21, May 1967, p. 28.

eight years in the case of machinery and over 20 years in the case of barns and other structures. In September 1967, a Soviet economist criticized the low rate of interest for its failure to stimulate the most productive use of the credit extended. Further, he criticized the even lower rate of interest—one-half of 1 per cent annually—paid on capital funds that collective farms deposited in the State Bank. He strongly favored a higher rate that would give the farms greater incentive to increase funds kept in the Bank.[13]

[13] *Izvestia*, September 15, 1967.

# Labor in the Soviet Economy

# 6

Since the beginning of Stalinist industrialization in the late 1920's, there have been major quantitative and qualitative changes in the Soviet labor force itself and in the conditions in which it has worked. The enormous growth in Soviet production during these years was in large part the result of the sharp increase both in the size of the labor force and in its productivity. A striking feature has been the massive shift of the Soviet work force from agricultural to non-agricultural occupations. In 1926, roughly 80 per cent of all Soviet workers were engaged in agriculture; forty years later that figure was down to about 33 per cent. The great qualitative upgrading of the Soviet work force has been largely the result of the enormous investment in education and training. In 1928, for example, the Soviet economy employed only 233,000 university-trained specialists. In the late 1960's, it employed over 5,000,000. These upward trends were reversed temporarily during 1941-1945 when World War II claimed tens of millions of victims. Nevertheless, despite the massive setback during that conflict, subsequent development made the Soviet labor force of the late 1960's the largest, the best educated, and the most skilled in that nation's history.

In the late 1960's the Soviet labor force consisted of some 125-130,000,000 people, perhaps 50 per cent more than in 1926. But the agricultural labor force in the late 1960's was less than 45,000,000 people as compared to 71,000,000 in 1926. The non-agricultural labor force in the late 1960's numbered about 80-85,000,000 people; it had been less than 15,000,000 forty years earlier. Put another way, over more than forty years of intensive industrialization, the Soviet farm labor force declined almost 40 per cent; the non-farm labor force increased between five and six times.[1]

Women have always played an important role in the Soviet work force, but their role has been particularly vital in the years since millions of able-bodied men were killed in World War II. In 1959, 51.9 per cent of the Soviet labor force consisted of women. They accounted for 61.5 per cent of the agricultural labor force and 44.2 per cent of the non-agricultural labor force.[2] Even as late as 1966 there were more women than men workers in the Soviet economy. In that year, women accounted for 70-86 per cent of all Soviet workers in medical care, education, trade, restaurant, banking and insurance institutions; 47 per cent of the industrial labor force; and even 28 per cent of the construction labor force.[3] In the Soviet Union one finds many women physicists, engineers, chemists, and doctors. One finds even more women employed as ditch diggers, street cleaners, and other manual laborers. At the height of the Soviet labor shortage during and after World War II, there were many Soviet women working as longshoremen and coal miners, and in other capacities where their employment would be unthinkable in Western Europe or the United States.

Historically, central planning for the mobilization and distribution of labor as well as centralized wage control have been key areas of Soviet economic planning. Balances of labor supply and requirements are still important components of Soviet economic plans, along with the similar balances of supply and requirements of important metals, chemicals, and machinery. In earlier years,

---

[1] Comparisons made on the basis of data in *New Directions in the Soviet Economy*, p. 746; Frank Lorimer, *The Population of the Soviet Union: History and Prospects.* (Geneva: League of Nations, 1946), p. 100; and Norton T. Dodge, *Women in the Soviet Economy* (Baltimore: The Johns Hopkins Press, 1966). p. 44.

[2] Dodge, *op. cit.*, p. 44.

[3] *Strana Sovetov za 50 Let*, p. 235.

Soviet planners fixed maximum limits on the number of workers who might be employed at each enterprise. They also handed down directives on average and total wages in each plant. Under the new economic system adopted in 1965, this kind of detailed control has been abandoned. Only the total wage fund of an enterprise must be approved from above or set by higher authority. Nevertheless, the labor sections of the national and republic economic plans remain important as authorities seek to assure the availability of the requisite numbers of skilled and unskilled workers needed to meet the nation's production targets. This central planning of labor resources also guides the extensive vocational training and educational systems of the Soviet Union. These training efforts seek to assure that adequate numbers of specialists of different kinds—from nurses and electricians to mathematicians and nuclear physicists—are available when and where they are needed. Ideally, Soviet labor planning should eliminate both problems of labor surplus and of labor shortage. The oft-repeated claim that there is no Soviet unemployment is in essence the assertion that Soviet planning eliminates labor surpluses and, therefore, involuntary unemployment.

Soviet planning has been as imperfect in this area as in others. In the 1960's, the Soviet Union has suffered simultaneously from local surpluses and local shortages of labor in different areas. Unemployment as the West understands the term has even become enough of a problem to be the subject of repeated cautious public discussion. Soviet labor shortages have been most severe in the areas of rapidly growing labor demand, especially in regions of Siberia where the severity of climate and the lack of suitable housing and other living needs have made workers reluctant to take—or to hold—jobs. The unemployment problem has been very serious in the mid- and late 1960's for young people leaving school without a skill that is in demand, and also for women in small and medium-sized cities where the structure of industry has not been such as to provide job openings for females. In addition, of course, the Soviet Union has both frictional and seasonal unemployment. A Soviet worker who is fired or who quits does not normally get a job the very next day. Often he must look for several weeks or even for months before he can get a satisfactory place. Also, industries with pronounced seasonal patterns of operations—for example, lumbering and fishing—create problems of seasonal unemployment in the Soviet Union as elsewhere. The propaganda claim that there is no unemployment brought two adverse consequences: the Soviet Union has no unemployment compensation for those without jobs, and until recently it had no national system of labor exchanges or employment offices to help bring jobs and job seekers together. There has been increasing pressure for such a system of labor exchanges in recent years, and the problem of *trudoustroistvo*—job placement—is now discussed widely. [4]

A beginning is being made toward meeting these problems. Thus in December 1966 each Soviet republic was instructed to set up a State Committee on Labor Resource Utilization. The committees are charged with informing the public about available jobs, with taking measures to retrain surplus workers and redistribute them to areas and enterprises needing laborers, as well as with assuming general responsibilities for labor recruitment and labor resettlement. The *Gosplan's* Labor Resources Department was put in charge of these new organizations. Complaints published in the Soviet press in 1968 indicated that the local employment offices set up by this new agency had by no means yet ended confusion in the Soviet labor market.

The amount of labor available in the Soviet Union depends not only upon the number of people who work, but also upon the number of hours they work. During World War II, millions in Soviet industry, transport, and trade worked 60 or 66 hours weekly. After the war, the basic work week was set at 48 hours, consisting of 6 work days of 8 hours each. In 1956, this was cut to 46 hours by reducing Saturday work hours to 6; by 1960 other decrees reduced Monday-to-Friday work hours from 8 to 7, with a resultant basic work week of 41 hours. In 1967, to mark the fiftieth anniversary of the Bolshevik Revolution, the Soviet basic work week was changed from 6 to 5 work days, but the 41-hour week was maintained by increasing daily working hours. Those who work underground or in especially hazardous occupations have shorter daily and weekly hours, as do workers in the 15-17 age bracket. This is significant progress, but it has been slower and less than Khrushchev promised in the Seven Year Plan for 1959-1965. His promise in 1959 was that Soviet workers would have a 40-hour week by 1962, and that by 1964 they would start shifting to a 35-hour week. [5]

---

[4] Emily Clark Brown, *Soviet Trade Unions and Labor Relations* (Cambridge: Harvard University Press, 1966), Chapter II. *Labor Developments Abroad,* November 1965, pp. 1-3.

[5] *Pravda,* January 28, 1959.

## The Easing of Soviet Labor Controls

The most important change in Soviet labor relations since Stalin's death has been the wholesale retreat from the compulsion and coercion that dominated Stalin's rule—especially from the late 1930's to 1953. During that period millions of prisoner laborers received extremely brutal treatment which Soviet novelist Alexander Solzhenitsyn described so vividly in his justly celebrated book, *One Day in the Life of Ivan Denisovich*. Many of these slave workers were former *kulaks*, Soviet veterans of World War II who had been German prisoners during that conflict, clergymen, and real or suspected political dissidents. But even the nominally free workers in Soviet factories and mines worked under near-serf rules during these years. Under threat of prison sentence for violators, workers were prohibited from changing their jobs without employer consent and from being absent from work without medical or similar authorization. Repeated late arrival at work was also a punishable crime. Young people of 14 to 17 were liable to be drafted for state-assigned vocational training. Skilled workers and technicians could be transferred anywhere in the country regardless of their wishes. Workers were issued "labor books" which their employer kept and without which they could not be legally hired. The employer, of course, returned a worker's *trudovaya kniga* (labor book) only if he were fired or were authorized to leave his job. In railroad transport during these years, workers were under the rigors of military discipline with correspondingly severe penalties for infractions. [6]

Soviet unions in the Stalinist period did nothing to defend their members against the state. Completely dominated by the Communist party, these unions saw their primary function as that of helping to increase production and productivity. In practice, strikes were forbidden and union officials acted as tools of management in seeking to restrain worker discontent. In these circumstances, workers dissatisfied with working and living conditions in a plant had no escape except to try to shift jobs with the hope that another factory or mine would be better. This situation produced a high labor turnover which Stalin sought to check by his law requiring workers to stay at their jobs. [7]

---

[6] Schwartz, *Russia's Soviet Economy*, pp. 524-25.

[7] Arvid Broderson, *The Soviet Worker* (New York: Random House, Inc., 1966), pp. 79-83.

The great bulk of this severe labor control legislation and system was liquidated in the mid-1950's, within five years after Stalin's death. In this period, for example, most slave laborers were released; many of them were given judicial certificates recognizing their alleged political crimes as fabrications. A decree of March 8, 1956 ended the imposition of prison sentences on persons leaving their jobs or playing hookey from work without authorization. It also permitted workers to quit if they gave two weeks advance notice. Even earlier, on March 18, 1955, another decree ended the draft of teen-agers for vocational training. But the labor book was retained, and, in 1961, legislation was passed providing imprisonment for "parasites," defined as "able bodied adult citizens who avoid socially useful work and derive unearned income from the exploitation of land plots, automobiles or housing" and "persons who take jobs . . . only for the sake of appearance and live on funds obtained by nonlabor means."[8]

The decree which ended criminal penalties for unauthorized quitting of jobs had two important effects. One was a sudden upward surge in labor turnover. In 1950, 15 per cent of all Soviet industrial workers and 18 per cent of all construction workers left their jobs voluntarily or were fired for infractions of labor discipline. In 1956, the corresponding figure in industry was 38 per cent, but this had dropped to 20 per cent by 1962. The construction labor turnover figure was 41 per cent in 1960.[9] A second result was the renewal of serious Soviet research to determine the causes of labor turnover. These studies found that much of this expensive shifting from job to job reflected dissatisfaction with wages, with working conditions, and/or with living conditions. By the mid-1960's, official Soviet concern with the impact of high labor turnover was so great that measures aimed at introducing compulsory bans against unauthorized quitting were again under serious consideration. In late 1966 a Central Committee resolution denounced poor labor discipline and demanded intensified Communist party activity and other local measures to end the resultant great loss of working time. The resolution nominally concerned only one region, Tula Province, but there could be little

---

[8] Edmund Nash, "Recent Changes in Labor Controls in the Soviet Union," in *New Directions in the Soviet Economy*, pp. 851-58.

[9] Murray Feshbach, "Manpower in the USSR: A Survey of Recent Trends and Prospects," in *New Directions in the Soviet Economy*, p. 732.

doubt that the problem was national in scope.[10] For example, here is how an authoritative Soviet periodical described the situation in November 1966:

> For the overwhelming majority of members of our society which is moving toward Communism, labor has been converted from a simple means of existence into a person's first vital requirement. However, it is impossible to close eyes to the fact that there are still people among us who do not want to work honorably, who are without conscience in fulfilling their obligations before society, and who play truant from work and commit other violations of labor discipline and order. The work of strengthening labor discipline has far from everywhere been put in necessary order. Individual economic directors, the party and union organizations of enterprises and construction projects do not carry on persistent struggles with the disorganizers of production, do not apply against them all the force of social action and insufficiently use the measures provided by Soviet law.[11]

Addressing the 14th Congress of the Soviet trade union movement on February 27, 1968, the Chairman of the All-Union Central Council of Trade Unions, Alexander N. Shelepin, made these comments on the problem of labor discipline:

> The successes of social production depend to a large extent on the permanence of the staff of cadres. But necessary attention to this is often lacking. Annually, a relatively large group of workers—chiefly young workers—changes places of employment. Union central committees, working jointly with ministries and departments, must deeply study the concrete causes of labor turnover at enterprises and by all means obtain their removal. Special attention must be paid to the strictest observance of labor and state discipline.
>
> The overwhelming majority of Soviet people work honestly and self sacrificingly. But there are still many facts of violations of labor discipline: unjustified absence from or lateness in coming to work, disorderly conduct at work, nonfulfillment of orders and instructions. Recently, in connection with the decision of the Communist party Central Committee on the work of the Tula province party organization in strengthening labor discipline, trade unions have improved their work in this respect. However, many union organizations still pay little attention to this problem.

---

[10] *Pravda*, December 22, 1966.
[11] *Ekonomicheskaya Gazeta*, No. 47, November 1966, p. 3.

## Soviet Wages

A key feature of the economic reform of 1965 is the effort to increase the incentive effect of Soviet wages. The goal is not new, of
course. Stalin was a firm advocate of wage incentives. He sought
to stimulate worker productivity and production by creating a
system in which there were wide wage and earnings differentials,
depending upon the different occupations and productivity per-
formances of individual workers. In the Stalin era, emphasis was
put upon piece wages with substantial bonuses paid for output in
excess of production norms. In a particular factory, the extremes
of wage inequality would be reflected in the difference between
the director's high salary and the minuscule wage of the cleaning
woman; it would also be reflected in the wide difference in earnings between a few "Stakhanovites" or "shock workers" and the
majority of their fellows. Under Stalin, wages tended to be high
in heavy industries such as coal mining or steel production and
low in service industries where teachers, doctors and the like received abysmally low salaries. This system undoubtedly had some
incentive effect, but it also had important negative consequences.
Since a worker's bonus depended upon output in excess of his
norm, there was much pressure—often successful despite government opposition—to have low norms set so that workers could be
assured bonuses for overfulfillment. The emphasis on piece rates
tended to encourage sloppy work aimed more at quantity than at
quality. Accompanying these Stalinist efforts to provide wage incentives, of course, was a system of "moral incentives" built
about the practice of publicizing and glorifying individual workers whose high production records were set up as models for
others. Enterprises also participated in "socialist competitions"
whose winners were decided by production performance.

The Khrushchev era—from the mid-1950's to 1964—introduced
significant deviations from the Stalinist pattern of wage policy.
Inequality of earnings was appreciably reduced, both by cutting
some of the highest salaries and incomes and, even more important, by raising the disgracefully low wages at the bottom. Thus,
in 1956, monthly minimum wages for those on the Soviet government payroll were raised to 27 rubles in rural areas and 30 rubles
in urban areas, and by 1965 they had been raised again to 40 and
45 rubles respectively. In September 1967 it was announced that
on January 1, 1968, the minimum monthly wage would be increased to 60 rubles.

In the late 1950's and early 1960's, a new organization, the
State Committee on Labor and Wages, carried out a massive re-

form of the Soviet wage system. Instead of the earlier great number of wage scales differing from factory to factory and industry to industry, a small number of wage scales was set up, aimed at insuring equal pay for equal work. The new Soviet wage system sought to increase work norms, while making more of each worker's pay come from his basic wage so as to ease the pressure for lower work norms. The spread between the lowest and highest wage rates in each industry was narrowed, and at the same time differentials in wages among industries were set to reflect the relative importance of different industries as well as the discomfort and danger of conditions of work in different occupations. In July 1964, Premier Khrushchev announced that during the preceding five years 50,000,000 workers had received wage increases of 13-25 per cent, costing 4.5 billion rubles annually. At the same time he announced an ambitious program for providing an average 21 per cent wage increase for 18,000,000 low paid service workers—doctors, teachers, barbers, clerks, janitors, nurses, and public utility repair men. He estimated the annual cost of these increases at 3.3 billion rubles![12]The factor that made these wage increases possible was, of course, the increasing productivity and production of the Soviet economy.

**TABLE 8.**   Soviet Workers' Average Earnings, 1940-1967

| Year | Average Monthly Money Earnings | Average Monthly Money Earnings plus Social Benefits |
|------|-------------------------------|-----------------------------------------------------|
|      | (*rubles*)                    |                                                     |
| 1940 | 33.0  | 40.6  |
| 1946 | 47.5  | 62.4  |
| 1950 | 63.9  | 82.4  |
| 1955 | 71.5  | 91.8  |
| 1960 | 80.1  | 107.7 |
| 1964 | 90.1  | 120.8 |
| 1965 | 95.6  | 129.0 |
| 1966 | 99.0  | 133.0 |
| 1967 | 103.7 | 139.5 |

In early 1966—after a hiatus of a quarter of a century—the Soviet Government ended its secrecy with regard to comprehensive wage data and began to publish them again. These data were published in two variants: average monthly money earnings; and average monthly earnings plus allowance for such benefits as the

---

[12] Schwartz, *The Soviet Economy Since Stalin*, pp. 100-102 and 178-79. Nash, *op. cit.*, pp. 859-60.

public education system, socialized medicine, pensions, and social insurance. The data are given in Table 8.[13]

Between 1940 and 1967 average Soviet monthly money wages more than tripled, while between 1950 and 1966 they increased more than 50 per cent. But, as we shall see, a part of these gains since 1940 has been lost to inflation. Moreover, even in 1967, Soviet money earnings were at a level equivalent, at the official ruble-dollar conversion ratio, to less than $30 a week.

Differences in earnings among different major economic fields, ranked in descending order of 1958 monthly money earnings, are shown by the data for 1958, 1965, and 1967.[14]

TABLE 9.    Earnings Differentials in the Soviet
Economy, 1958, 1965, and 1967

| Branch of Economy | 1958 | 1965 | 1967 |
|---|---|---|---|
| | | (rubles) | |
| Science and scientific services | 105.9 | 115.6 | 122.0 |
| Industry | 87.1 | 103.3 | 111.7 |
| Construction | 86.6 | 109.4 | 118.1 |
| Government administration | 84.2 | 104.7 | 112.5 |
| Transportation | 82.2 | 105.5 | 115.0 |
| Credit and insurance | 72.1 | 86.0 | 93.0 |
| Education | 69.4 | 93.6 | 96.5 |
| Medical services | 58.9 | 78.9 | 82.4 |
| Trade and restaurants | 58.1 | 74.9 | 82.5 |
| Communications | 58.0 | 73.9 | 78.0 |
| Housing and public utilities | 55.3 | 71.8 | 78.6 |
| State farms | 53.1 | 74.1 | 84.1 |

The policy Soviet wage planners followed during this period is suggested by the fact that between 1958 and 1967 workers in science received an average wage increase of 15 per cent, while the lowest groups, state farm workers and housing and public utility workers, got increases of about 60 and 40 per cent respectively. But at least one group of Soviet workers who were relatively well paid in 1958 were generously treated thereafter. Workers in water transport—sailors—had their average monthly wages raised from 97.9 rubles in 1958 to 142.5 rubles in 1967, a gain of almost 50 per cent.

Soviet sensitivity to the issue of wage differentials was interestingly shown by the Communist party Central Committee decision

---

[13] *Narkhoz 1965*, p. 567, and *Pravda*, January 29, 1967 and January 25, 1968.

[14] *Narkhoz 1965*, pp. 567-68. See also *Strana Sovetov za 50 Let*, p. 227.

of September 26, 1967 to raise the minimum wage to 60 rubles monthly. For some unspecified categories of workers the minimum wage and salary level was simultaneously raised to 70 rubles monthly. At the same time those workers receiving 61-80 rubles a month, and therefore presumably most conscious of the fact that lower paid workers had had their wages raised, were given a small increase in take home pay by having their marginal income tax rates reduced an average of 25 per cent. Finally, skilled workers operating machine tools in machinery and metal working plants were told they would get an average 15 per cent pay raise during the first half of 1968.

The use of wage differentials as a stimulus to attract workers to otherwise unattractive work areas was stressed by the same Central Committee decision to provide additional wage bonuses for those willing to work in the Soviet Far East and European North. The decision made *all* workers in these areas eligible for bonus pay, rather than limiting the higher rates to miners and other heavy industry workers as was done earlier. In areas such as Magadan and Kamchatka provinces, important gold mining and fishing centers, the decision provided a 10 per cent increase every six months until the bonus pay reached 100 per cent of the base pay or 300 rubles monthly.

To get some idea of changes in real wages and earnings, we must look at the evolution of the retail price level of the Soviet Union. Most Soviet retail trade takes place in state-owned stores in urban communities and in consumer cooperative stores in rural areas. Both types of establishments sell their wares at government-set prices that have been changed very rarely between the mid-1950's and the late 1960's. The only other major centers of retail trade are the free collective farm markets in cities and towns, where collective farms and farmers sell their surplus produce at prices determined by supply and demand. The prices of food sold in these free markets are normally much higher than the state prices. Soviet consumers are willing to pay the higher free market prices in part because the food sold there is fresher and of better quality than in the state stores, and in part because food can be bought in the free market when its supply at the lower price in state stores has been exhausted. In 1940 collective farm market prices were on the average 2.2 times the level of state prices for the same foods; in 1960 they were 1.35 times as high; and in 1964 1.63 times as high.[15] The data in Table 10 show

---

[15] *New Directions in the Soviet Economy*, p. 514.

the movement of state retail prices for all goods, of collective farm market prices for food, and of an index of all Soviet retail prices which has been weighted to take into account the fact that collective farm trade is now less than 5 per cent of all Soviet retail trade. The levels of the year 1950 are taken as 100 for each series. [16]

**TABLE 10.**   Soviet Retail Price Changes, 1940-1965

| Year | State Retail Prices | Free Market Prices | Overall Retail Price Index |
|---|---|---|---|
| 1940 | 54 | 102 | 58 |
| 1950 | 100 | 100 | 100 |
| 1955 | 74 | 116 | 76.6 |
| 1960 | 75 | 108 | 76.3 |
| 1964 | 76 | 138 | 79.5 |
| 1965 | 75 | 131 | 79 |

We can now obtain a measure of Soviet real wages by dividing the average monthly money wages by the overall retail price index as done in the following table.

**TABLE 11.**   Soviet Money Wages and Real Wages, 1940-1965

| Year | Monthly Money Wages | Overall Retail Price Index (1950 = 100) | Real Wages (1950 prices) |
|---|---|---|---|
| 1940 | 33.0 | 58 | 57 |
| 1950 | 63.9 | 100 | 63.9 |
| 1955 | 71.5 | 76.6 | 93 |
| 1960 | 80.1 | 76.3 | 105 |
| 1964 | 90.1 | 79.5 | 113 |
| 1965 | 95.6 | 79 | 121 |

The overall conclusion that Soviet real wages almost doubled between 1950 and 1965 does not seem unreasonable. It is notable that the most rapid pace of improvement was between 1950 and 1955, while the gain in 1965 alone was as great as that between 1960 and 1964, the period of slowest advance.

[16] Indexes of state retail and free market prices taken or computed from data in *Narkhoz 1958, 1961,* and *1965.* The free market price index is spliced together from two separate indexes, one based on a sample of 71 large cities and the other of 251 cities. The overall retail price index for 1950-1964 is taken from *New Directions in the Soviet Economy,* p. 526. The 1940 and 1965 figures have been estimated by the author.

The 1965 Soviet economic reform seeks to increase the incentive effect of the Soviet wage system by adding a new element to the long list of customary Soviet wage incentive devices—piece rates, bonuses for overfulfillment of production norms, bonuses for economy in the use of scarce material, and so on. The reform requires that a significant fraction of each worker's wage depend upon his enterprise's success in fulfilling its sales and profits plan. There had been limited profit sharing in the past when a so-called enterprise fund was set up from profits to pay bonuses and for other purposes. The reform seeks to make much larger amounts available for bonuses dependent upon profit, and thus to make profit sharing a far more potent incentive for good work and for cost cutting than it has been in the past. Bonuses under the reform will come both from the old wages fund of an enterprise and from the new material incentives fund derived from profits. An interesting point is the fact that, according to a Soviet source, before the reform industrial workers' earnings were almost independent of the overall production performance of the factory or mine they worked in.[17] Complaints voiced during the first two years after the introduction of the economic reform indicated that funds available for wage bonuses were still not as high as many felt necessary to provide adequate incentives.

## Soviet Trade Unions

Like many other Soviet institutions, the Soviet trade union movement, which has over 80,000,000 members in the late 1960's, has been substantially affected by the trends of the post-Stalin era. Under Stalin, Soviet unions were essentially company unions used by the state to control the mass of workers. Since Stalin's death, the unions have gained greater independence and have more ability to defend their members' interests. But they are still far from being the kind of workers organizations that unions are in the United States or Western Europe.

From the late 1920's to the early 1950's, Soviet unions were completely dominated by the drive to increase labor productivity and overall production. In every enterprise, union officials were essentially instruments of management, seeking to raise worker morale and to provide incentives that would produce harder and better work. Since these officials handled the distribution of social security and social insurance benefits, directed extensive recreation facilities, and had much to say about the distribution of

[17] *Sotsialistichesky Trud*, October 1965, p. 7.

housing and the like, they could favor good workers and punish poor ones. Even in these years, unions were nominally charged with protecting workers' interests. But it was taken for granted that they would never organize a strike, would oppose slowdowns, would put the needs of production ahead of workers' grievances, and would never complain about wage levels set by the state.

Inevitably, Soviet workers came to understand that they could not look to their unions for effective defense of their interests. The attitudes born of that understanding served in turn to weaken union effectiveness in spurring workers to higher productivity. Thus when Stalin's successors turned to the problem of revitalizing Soviet unions, they realized that these organizations had to become more effective defenders of workers' interests at the grassroots level if they were to have the prestige required to stimulate productivity. Here is the way Khrushchev put the new line for union officials at the 20th Soviet Communist party Congress in 1956:[18]

> The chief thing that our trade union bodies, including the Central Council of Trade Unions, lack is militancy in their work, creative excitement, businesslike attitudes, devotion to principle and initiative in raising basic, vital problems, whether measures for raising labor productivity or, let us say, problems of wages, housing and construction, of satisfying the daily needs of the workers and employees. It is well known that labor management contracts are concluded in enterprises. But on every hand there is failure to carry out these contracts, and the trade unions remain silent, as though everything was in order. Generally, it must be said that the unions have stopped having arguments with the managers; peace and harmony between them reign supreme. Yet, after all, when the interests of the cause are at stake, one should not be afraid to spoil relations; sometimes it is even good to argue really hard.

The intent, of course, was not to make Soviet unions primarily organizations defending their members' interests against employers, but rather to correct a balance that had gone badly awry over the years of all-out Stalinist emphasis on production. An important step was announced in a December 1957 resolution of the Communist party Central Committee. This granted greater power both to the national union leadership and to factory union committees at the grassroots. The State Committee on Labor and

---

[18]  *Pravda*, February 15, 1956.

Wages was required to adopt its chief policy decisions jointly with the All-Union Central Council of Trade Unions, thus giving the latter at least a veto. Local union committees were given a similar veto power over the firing of any worker by management; they were authorized to express their opinions about proposed candidates for factory managerial positions; and their rights to participate in activities such as drawing up a factory's plan, setting wage categories for different jobs, and setting workers' production norms were strengthened. A charter defining the rights and privileges of union committees in enterprises was published in mid-1958. [19]

Also, in July 1958, Permanent Production Conferences were set up at Soviet factories, construction sites, and state farms to involve workers more deeply in the solution of problems facing management, especially uncovering reserves to help raise productivity. Composed of elected union, Communist party, and Young Communist League representatives, these groups of workers meet periodically with management representatives to discuss the enterprise's problems. An American investigator who studied the operation of these groups in the Soviet Union in 1959 and 1962 concluded that "many production conferences had become real forces in their enterprises," but also noted that in other enterprises "inertia, fear of change, or desire for the 'quiet life' often keeps the leadership on either side from making full use of the possibilities." [20] In early 1968 the head of all Soviet trade unions, A. N. Shelepin, reported that there were 138,000 production conferences with over 5,000,000 members. He reported that annually these production conferences accepted about 1,500,000 proposals, but he complained that not all of the proposals were put into effect. He endorsed the idea of creating similar groups in enterprises engaged in transportation, communications, trade, services, scientific research, and other branches of the economy. He also called for setting fixed time limits within which enterprise managements would be required to consider the proposals of production conferences. More generally, it seems likely that the reforms of 1956-1958 have varied widely in their impact throughout the Soviet Union, bringing more active union defense of workers'

---

[19] *KPSS o Profsoyuzakh* (Moscow: Profizdat, 1967), pp. 431-37. *Pravda,* July 16, 1958.

[20] Brown, *Soviet Trade Unions and Labor Relations,* pp. 251-56. See also *Pravda,* February 28, 1968.

rights (within permitted limits, of course) and more worker participation in management in some places and little or no change in others.

In early 1957, a new system was set up for handling enterprise disputes between one or several workers and management, replacing an earlier procedure dating back to 1928. In the new system, disputes are brought before a factory (or shop) commission on labor disputes consisting of equal numbers of management and labor representatives. Ideally a decision is reached by agreement between both sides; but if the parties cannot agree, the dispute is brought to the union committee of the factory. A worker dissatisfied with the commission's decision may appeal to the People's Court, the local Soviet judicial organ. Management cannot appeal a decision by the joint commission since its representatives on that body have approved the decision. But the judgment on a labor dispute made by the factory union committee may be appealed by the management to the People's Court if the management believes the decision contradicts existing legislation. The joint commissions on labor disputes can handle disputes about work norms, wage categories for a given job, transfers of workers from one job to another, and similar low level matters. The commissions cannot handle disputes about basic wage rates or salary schedules, changes in the size of the work force, allocation of housing space, and matters affecting managerial personnel of the plant.[21]

## Collective Farmers' Incomes

We will conclude our discussion of labor conditions in the Soviet economy with a brief treatment of collective farmers' incomes, a subject on which Soviet statisticians have been reticent in the past. Collective farmers are paid both in money and in farm products for their work on the *kolkhoz* fields. They also receive income from the produce grown on their private plots. In the 1950's and 1960's the number of collective farmers has been declining, partly because of migration to non-farm work and partly because of the trend toward turning the poorest *kolkhozy* into state farms. Since Stalin's death, collective farm money incomes have risen rapidly both because of increased output and, even more, because of sharply increased prices paid by the state

---

[21] The regulations on the procedure for examining labor disputes, approved January 31, 1957, are given in *Spravochnik Profsoyuznogo Rabotnika 1967* (Moscow: Profizdat, 1967), pp. 282-92.

for agricultural produce. Moreover, there has been a trend over these years toward paying a larger percentage of the collective farmers' wages in money.

The result of these developments has been a very large increase in the average annual money wages received by collective farmers, as indicated by the data in the table.[22]

**TABLE 12.** Earnings of Soviet Collective Farmers, 1950-1965

| Year | Total Collective Farm Wage Payments (billion rubles) | Average Number of Collective Farmers (millions) | Average Annual Money Wage (rubles) |
|------|------------------------------------------------------|-------------------------------------------------|------------------------------------|
| 1950 | 1.18 | 25.1 | 47 |
| 1955 | 3.06 | 22.1 | 139 |
| 1960 | 4.94 | 20.1 | 247 |
| 1965 | 8.62 | 17.6 | 489 |

The more than ten-fold increase in average annual money wages between 1950 and 1965 suggests that very real progress has been made in improving the economic fortunes of collective farmers. But even as late as 1965 the average monthly money wage of a collective farmer was still only 40 rubles, less than half his urban counterpart's wage. The rapidly diminishing portion of the collective farmer's wage paid in kind can hardly have done much to reduce this great difference in compensation. These generally low wages provided a major source of pressure for flight from the farms to the factories in the Soviet Union. It should be noted that these data reflect neither the 1966 decision to equalize the earnings of collective farm and state farm workers nor the September 1967 decision to establish a minimum wage in 1968 of 60 rubles a month. Some available evidence suggests that collective farmers' labor earnings during the two-year period 1966-1967 may have risen about 20 per cent above the 1965 level.

The Soviet government's realization of the importance of narrowing the income difference between agricultural and non-agricultural workers was revealed in the Eighth Five Year Plan. This provided for collective farm workers' incomes (monetary and in kind) in 1970 to be 38 per cent higher than in 1965, a rise almost

---

[22] Total wage payments data are mainly estimates from *New Directions in the Soviet Economy*, p. 526. Number of collective farmers from *Narkhoz 1965*. p. 435, and *Selskoye Khozyaistvo SSSR* (Moscow: Gosstatizdat, 1960), p. 451. Average annual wage obtained by division.

twice that provided for government workers and employees during the same period. According to Politburo member Dmitry Polyansky, already in 1966 the national average earnings of a collective farmer exceeded three rubles per working day, 14 per cent above 1965. Mr. Polyansky, in an article published in October 1967, came close to outlining a program for trying to equalize the earnings and status of collective farmers with urban workers. He raised the prospect of collective farmers becoming "members of trade unions" able "to avail themselves of the same rights as trade union members to receive social insurance benefits." He spoke of extending the five-day work week to agricultural work, and he stressed the importance of trying to give all able-bodied rural inhabitants year-round employment in communal production. Finally, he strongly backed the use of state funds to help improve housing and other amenities in rural areas, arguing that "urban-type collective farm villages cannot be created by individual construction. Not only collective farm, but also government funds and the organization of construction by industrial methods will be needed to do this."[23]

[23] *Kommunist*, No. 15, October 1967, pp. 15-31.

# The Soviet Union
# in the World Economy

# 7

Since 1945, the Soviet Union's increasing production has made
that country an ever more important factor in the world economy.
In the early years after World War II, the Soviet Union relied
heavily upon foreign resources to speed its recovery from the
great destruction of that conflict. Large amounts of machinery, raw
materials, livestock, and other essentials seized in the Soviet-oc-
cupied areas of Germany, Eastern Europe, Korea, and China
helped substantially to supplement the meager Soviet production
of those years. So did international relief supplies—food, medicine, agricultural essentials—provided by the United Nations Relief and Rehabilitation Administration, and by the goods the
United States shipped from what remained in the Lend-Lease
pipeline at the end of the actual fighting.

By the late 1960's, the Soviet Union had long since left behind
the era in which it had to loot conquered countries and receive
relief. Now, more than two decades after World War II, the Soviet Union is one of the world's major trading nations with an
annual foreign trade volume approaching $20 billion. It is one
of the world's great maritime and air transport powers. Soviet
ships sail all the seas, and Soviet planes fly passengers and freight

to almost all continents. Among other things, the Soviet Union is a growing factor in world tourism. Its banks in London, Paris, and other Western centers play appreciable roles in world financial markets. Further, the economic and technical assistance that country provides to underdeveloped countries in Asia, Africa, and Latin America makes the Soviet Union a closely watched competitor of the United States. Relations with the Soviet Union greatly influence the economic life of most Eastern European states, as well as of Cuba, North Vietnam, North Korea, and Mongolia. Last, but not least, the Soviet Union is the key member of the Council for Mutual Economic Assistance (Comecon) and other international economic institutions uniting the pro-Soviet nations in the Communist world. At any given moment in the late 1960's, thousands of Soviet citizens were abroad on economic and technical missions for their government while thousands of foreigners were in Moscow and other Soviet cities on similar business errands for their nations or for private firms in their countries. In 1966, for example, almost 12,000 Soviet technicians were working on economic aid projects in non-Communist underdeveloped nations.

As one might suppose, Soviet foreign economic relations are a closely integrated part of the overall Soviet government-owned, government-operated, and government-planned economy. Soviet foreign trade is a state monopoly, challenged only in a small way by smugglers. Soviet organizations engaged in foreign trade act as both export and import agents for Soviet domestic enterprises. Frequently Soviet foreign economic relations are dominated by political considerations. This is particularly true, of course, in the foreign aid field where such assistance is a means of political penetration and influence. But Soviet economic power has also been used to punish recalcitrant nations. China, Albania, Yugoslavia, Finland, and Israel are only some of the countries that have experienced the severe impact of Soviet employment of actual or threatened trade reduction as a weapon of political warfare. As recently as December 1967, the head of the Rumanian Communist party hinted publicly that the Soviet Union was using trade as a means of exerting political pressure on his country. From time to time, also, charges have been made that the Soviet government deliberately dumped commodities on the world market—for example, grain in the early 1930's, oil, aluminum, and tin in the late 1950's—in order to disorganize existing price structures. Nevertheless, in most cases Soviet foreign trade with non-Communist countries is dominated by the desire to sell for as high a price as possible and to buy for as low a price as possible.

The growth, in value terms, and the changing geographic distribution of Soviet foreign trade between Communist and non-Communist countries in representative years since World War II is shown in the table below. [1] In 1967, we may note, total Soviet foreign trade turnover amounted to about 16.4 billion rubles or more than $18 billion.

**TABLE 13.**    Soviet Foreign Trade with Communist and Non-Communist Countries since 1946

| | *1946* | *1952* | *1959* | *1966* | *1967* |
|---|---|---|---|---|---|
| | | *(billions of rubles)* | | | |
| Foreign Trade Turnover | 1.3 | 4.8 | 9.5 | 15.1 | 16.4 |
| With Communist Countries | .7 | 3.9 | 7.1 | 10.0 | 11.1 |
| With Non-Communist Countries | .6 | 1.1 | 2.4 | 5.1 | 5.3 |
| Exports | .6 | 2.5 | 4.9 | 8.0 | 8.7 |
| To Communist Countries | .4 | 2.1 | 3.7 | 5.3 | 5.7 |
| To Non-Communist Countries | .2 | .4 | 1.2 | 2.7 | 3.0 |
| Imports | .7 | 2.3 | 4.6 | 7.1 | 7.7 |
| From Communist Countries | .4 | 1.8 | 3.4 | 4.7 | 5.4 |
| From Non-Communist Countries | .3 | .5 | 1.2 | 2.4 | 2.3 |

Sources: Official Soviet Statistics.

Over the 21-year period from 1946 to 1967, the value of Soviet foreign trade grew more than 12 times. In 1946, only little more than half of Soviet trade was with other Communist countries. By 1952, that proportion had grown to about 80 per cent, in part because of the rigorous embargo against strategic exports to the Soviet Union maintained by key Western countries. Even in 1959 about three-quarters of Soviet trade was still with other Communist countries, but by 1966 that proportion had fallen to about two-thirds. Indicative of the strong trend toward increased trade with non-Communist countries is the fact that between 1959 and 1966 this commerce more than doubled. In the same period, however, the value of Soviet trade with other Communist countries increased only about 40 per cent. Behind this trend toward rapid growth of Soviet trade with capitalist countries has been the easing of East-West tensions and the consequent rapid dismant-

---

[1] *Narkhoz 1962*, p. 548. *SSSR v Tsifrakh v 1967 godu*, p. 34.

ling of the West's earlier controls on and barriers to trade with
the Soviet Union.

The influence of political as well as economic forces upon
the growth of Soviet trade with different countries can be seen
by looking at the changes in this commerce in recent years. Let
us begin by looking at the key Communist trade partners of the
Soviet Union. [2]

TABLE 14.    Soviet Trade with Other Communist-
ruled Nations, 1958, 1965, 1966,
and 1967

| Country | | Total Trade° | | |
|---------|------|------|------|------|
| | 1958 | 1965 | 1966 | 1967 |
| | | (million rubles) | | |
| China | 1364 | 376 | 287 | 96 |
| East Germany | 1454 | 2384 | 2380 | 2546 |
| Czechoslovakia | 863 | 1764 | 1633 | 1755 |
| Poland | 577 | 1357 | 1383 | 1633 |
| Rumania | 436 | 759 | 713 | 737 |
| Hungary | 326 | 955 | 915 | 1064 |
| Bulgaria | 363 | 1084 | 1216 | 1382 |
| Mongolia | 101 | 170 | 198 | 224 |
| Yugoslavia | 92 | 300 | 367 | 462 |
| North Korea | 95 | 160 | 160 | 197 |
| North Vietnam | 16 | 95 | 84 | 152 |
| Cuba | 14 | 646 | 689 | 842 |

° Exports plus imports.
Sources: Official Soviet Statistics.

Albania, China, and Cuba provide the most dramatic examples
of the relationship between politics and trade. Albanian trade
with the Soviet Union ended entirely after Premier Khrushchev's
bitter attack on that country's Communist leaders in October
1961. The same bitter political differences were the prime force
making for the 93 per cent decline in Soviet-Chinese trade between 1958 and 1967. Cuba, in 1958, was not yet a Communist-
ruled country, so the growth shown in the table reflects the economic consequences of that country's shift under Fidel Castro
from the non-Communist to the Communist camp and the resulting enormous Cuban economic dependence upon the Soviet
Union. The relatively modest growth of Rumanian-Soviet trade

[2] Data from *Vneshnyaya Torgovlya SSSR za 1962 god* (Moscow: Vneshtor-
gizdat, 1963), pp. 10-14, and the corresponding volume for 1965, pp. 10-15.
*United Nations Monthly Bulletin of Statistics*, June 1967, pp. xvi-xvii, and
*Vneshnyaya Torgovlya*, August 1967, and June, 1968.

since 1958 is in part the result of Rumania's increasing political independence. Conversely, the rapid increase in Soviet-Yugoslav trade followed a political rapprochement after 1960.

East Germany and Czechoslovakia, the Soviet Union's two leading trading partners, are in effect workshops for the Soviet Union, enormously dependent upon imported Soviet raw materials. In return, these two countries export machinery, chemicals, and relatively high quality consumer goods. Mongolia and Cuba, on the other hand, are dependent upon the Soviet Union for a very wide variety of machinery, chemicals, industrial raw materials, and even foodstuffs, while having only very limited sources of payment. The Mongolians send to Moscow mainly wool, cattle, and other livestock products, while the Cubans send primarily sugar. Since the escalation of the war in Vietnam in early 1965, of course, North Vietnam has been heavily dependent upon the Soviet Union for many things, particularly for modern military equipment, including planes, missiles, anti-aircraft guns, radar, and similar items. Soviet shipments of weapons to North Vietnam have been estimated by some sources to have reached a value of one billion dollars annually in 1966 and 1967. But these arms deliveries are not included in the trade data above.

**TABLE 15.**    Soviet Trade with Developed
Capitalist Nations, 1958, 1965, 1966,
and 1967

| Country | Total Trade° | | | |
|---|---|---|---|---|
| | 1958 | 1965 | 1966 | 1967 |
| | | (million rubles) | | |
| United States | 28 | 89 | 99 | 92 |
| Britain | 197 | 397 | 449 | 451 |
| West Germany | 124 | 248 | 292 | 319 |
| France | 151 | 202 | 261 | 300 |
| Italy | 66 | 225 | 224 | 348 |
| Finland | 229 | 405 | 426 | 461 |
| Japan | 34 | 326 | 417 | 467 |
| Canada | 25 | 240 | 325 | 147 |

° Exports plus imports.
Sources: Official Soviet Statistics.

We will consider next Soviet trade in recent years with the developed non-Communist industrial nations. The modest role of the United States in Soviet trade is primarily explained by the continued relative stringency of American controls over such commerce. Though President Johnson has made some important beginnings toward reducing the list of goods whose export is prohibited and toward easing American laws limiting or prohibiting credits to the Soviet Union, the United States regulations in this area still reflect much of the cold war era of the 1950's. The Western European countries have largely dropped the old controls—except for the most strategic goods—and they have been willing to extend credits to the Soviet Union. Japan has shown a similar willingness to trade and give credits. Hence, the sharp increase of Japanese and West European trade with the Soviet Union is mainly a reflection of the improved political atmosphere. Canada's rise as a trading partner of the Soviet Union is the result largely of Soviet wheat purchases. In 1963-1964 Soviet wheat purchases from the United States temporarily sent U.S.-Soviet trade up sharply. Finland's high volume of trade with the Soviet Union is a legacy of the former country's defeat in World War II. Its present extensive economic connections with Moscow reflect in part development of relationships begun with heavy reparations the Soviet Union imposed upon and collected from Finland after 1945. To meet its reparations obligations, Finland had to create a large volume of new productive capacity in industries previously non-existent or little developed there. When reparations payments ended, these new Finnish industries remained heavily dependent on Soviet markets.

In its economic relations with Western Europe and Japan, the Soviet Union's trade pattern resembles more that of an underdeveloped country than the world's second largest industrial power. In effect, this trade consists mainly of Soviet raw materials being exchanged for Western European and Japanese machinery, chemicals, and manufactured goods. In 1965, for example, the bulk of Soviet exports to Japan consisted of coal, petroleum, pig iron, lumber, non-ferrous metals, and cotton. Of Soviet imports from Japan, however, machinery and ships accounted for over 40 per cent in value, pipe and other fabricated metal products for 20 per cent, and chemicals for more than 10 per cent. For the Soviet Union, Western Europe and Japan are particularly important as sources of advanced technology needed in the chemical, plastics, textile, and other civilian industries which have been neglected in the past during Soviet concentration on military needs. The $800,000,000 Soviet contract concluded in 1966 with Italy's Fiat motor company resulted from Soviet understanding that Western automobile production technology is far ahead of that of the Soviet Union. The automobile plant that Fiat is helping build at the town of Togliatti in the Volga Valley will be, when completed in the early 1970's, the largest and most modern Soviet motor car factory. Italy's willingness to provide liberal credit terms played an important role in making this huge contract possible. The very sharp 1967 increase in Soviet-Italian trade reflected the Soviet Union's rising role as a supplier of oil and other raw materials to Italy.

The Soviet need for capital from abroad has also been a major factor in Soviet negotiations with Japan during the 1960's. The Soviet government has been seeking to induce Japanese business firms to extend large credits to help finance the development of rich Soviet raw material resources in Siberia. The Soviet Union has proposed that repayment be made by export to Japan of raw materials produced at the new mines, oil wells, etc. One Japanese counter-proposal was discussed in Moscow in June 1967. This was an offer to ship $500,000,000 worth of Japanese construction machinery to the Soviet Union over a five-year period, in return for Soviet shipment to Japan during that time of lumber worth the same amount.[3]

Finally we turn to one of the most rapidly growing areas of Soviet foreign economic relations since the mid-1950's—trade with non-Communist underdeveloped countries. As late as 1955, this was only a tiny fraction of Soviet commerce. It was confined mainly to low levels of trade with such immediate neighbors as Iran, Turkey, and Afghanistan, and purchases of needed raw materials from a few more distant countries—natural rubber from Malaysia, livestock products from Argentina, and long staple cotton from Egypt. By 1960, the value of this trade exceeded $800,000,000 and accounted for about 7 per cent of all Soviet commerce. By 1966, this commerce exceeded $2 billion and accounted for 12 per cent of all Soviet foreign trade. In 1967, however, this trade remained almost stagnant, increasing only slightly to a total of $2.1 billion.[4]

Using 1955 as a base year for comparison, the growth of Soviet trade with its chief partners among the non-Communist underdeveloped countries is shown in Table 16.[5]

[3] *Financial Times,* June 16, 1967.
[4] *Vneshnyaya Torgovlya,* August 1967, and June 1968.
[5] *United Nations Monthly Bulletin of Statistics,* June 1967, and July 1968.

**TABLE 16.**  Soviet Trade with Developing
Nations, 1958, 1965, 1966, and 1967

| Country | Total Trade° (million rubles) | | | |
|---------|------|------|------|------|
|         | 1955 | 1965 | 1966 | 1967 |
| Egypt       | 24 | 335 | 314 | 348 |
| India       | 11 | 381 | 346 | 309 |
| Malaysia    | 20 | 101 | 113 | 87  |
| Argentina   | 47 | 83  | 104 | 25  |
| Afghanistan | 22 | 64  | 83  | 70  |
| Pakistan    | —  | 16  | 61  | 60  |
| Brazil      | 2  | 55  | 53  | 42  |
| Iran        | 37 | 30  | 46  | 84  |
| Turkey      | 12 | 32  | 42  | 50  |
| Ghana       | 10 | 59  | 35  | 30  |
| Iraq        | —  | 30  | 35  | 37  |
| Syria       | —  | 28  | 38  | 47  |
| Indonesia   | 3  | 78  | 32  | 27  |

° Exports plus imports.
Sources: Official Soviet Statistics.

In general these underdeveloped nations export raw materials
and foodstuffs to the Soviet Union which ships in return armaments, machinery, manufactured goods, medicines, and some Soviet raw materials, for example oil. The magnitude of Soviet arms
shipments to some of these countries was evidenced by the huge
amount of weapons captured by Israel from the Soviet-supplied
Egyptian and Syrian armies in June 1967, much of it very modern
artillery, tanks, missiles, radar, fighter planes, and even nuclear
decontamination equipment.[6] If necessary, the Soviet Union pays
in convertible currency. Malaysia, for example, sold almost $300
million worth of goods, mostly rubber, to the Soviet Union during 1964-1966, but bought almost nothing from that country. A
1967 agreement, however, provided for Malaysian purchases from
as well as sales to the Soviet Union.

Arms shipments aside, there have been important political and
economic reasons for the growth of Soviet trade with the underdeveloped countries since the mid-1950's. Politically, the Soviet
Union has sought increased influence in these nations. It has also
tried to use economic means to buttress pro-Soviet rulers in some
of these countries. Nasser in Egypt, Nkrumah in Ghana, and Sukarno in Indonesia are representative of the political figures
Moscow has sought to help. Not surprisingly, when some of these
leaders have fallen from power—as happened to Nkrumah and

[6] *New York Times*, June 27, 1967, p. 10.

Sukarno in the mid-1960's—that change has quickly been reflected in a diminution of economic relations with the Soviet Union. But the Soviet Union and the underdeveloped countries have also had economic reasons for expanded commerce. Moscow has sought markets in these countries for its manufactured products and in return looks to these countries for raw materials and tropical foodstuffs. The underdeveloped countries want markets for their products and can see advantages for themselves from stimulating rivalry between Soviet and Western suppliers. Iran is a major example of a country whose foreign trade has in the past been primarily with the West, but which is now turning toward greater economic relations with Moscow. Agreements negotiated in the mid-1960's envisage large scale shipments of Iranian natural gas to the Soviet Union via a new pipe line in return for Soviet aid in building an Iranian steel mill and otherwise helping Iran to industrialize. Soviet-Iranian trade in 1967 was almost double the value of that trade in 1966, reflecting the impact of these agreements.

The chief instrument of Soviet penetration into many other developing countries has been the extension of economic and technical aid financed by long term credits carrying very low interest rates, usually 2.5-3 per cent. The Aswan Dam, being built in Egypt with Soviet aid, is perhaps the most spectacular of these Soviet projects which include a major steel mill in India, roads and an airport in Afghanistan, factories of many kinds in different countries, and a wide variety of other installations. As of the beginning of 1968, a United States Congress study found that Soviet economic aid commitments since 1954 to 36 underdeveloped countries totaled about $6.0 billion. Actual deliveries to that time, however were much less. These credits help pay for Soviet machinery, for the services of Soviet experts sent to the recipient countries to design new plants or prospect for oil and other minerals, for training citizens of the recipient countries in Soviet educational institutions, and the like. Under the aid program thousands of Soviet experts have worked in many different countries, while tens of thousands of Asians, Africans, and Latin Americans have received training in Soviet schools, factories, and other institutions. In addition to economic aid, the Soviet Union is believed to have provided $4-4.5 billion in credits for military aid to less developed countries.

Soviet credits are also used as a commercial weapon to help open new markets for Soviet manufactures. In May 1967, for example, the Soviet Union offered Uruguay a trade credit of $20

million carrying 5 per cent annual interest and repayable in eight
years to finance the purchase of Soviet agricultural and industrial machinery. Some months earlier the Soviet Union had negotiated similar credits of $100 million for Brazil and $15 million
for Chile. In this period Soviet spokesmen were saying that corresponding offers would be made to many Latin American countries. The purpose, a Soviet spokesman said, was to offer Latin
Americans what he called a viable alternative to dependence on
the United States.[7] Soviet interest in expanding economic relations with Latin American countries having strongly anti-Com-
munist governments drew repeated fire from Fidel Castro in
1966 and 1967, but Moscow persisted nevertheless.

Similar credits for economic development have been extended
in the past, of course, to Communist-ruled countries. Those
countries have also received loans to finance arms purchases.
Soviet credits played a significant role in helping Chinese economic growth in the early 1950's, North Korean economic recovery
after the Korean War of 1950-1953, Hungarian economic recon-
struction after the Soviet repression of Hungary's 1956 revolution, Cuba's massive switch from dependence on the United
States to dependence on the Soviet Union in the 1960's, North
Vietnam's effort to conquer South Vietnam against American opposition in 1965 and afterward, and the industrialization of Mongolia. Where such Soviet credits are available, substantial trade
deficits can be financed by the recipient country as the data for
1966 in the following table show.[8]

**TABLE 17.**    Soviet Credit-Financed Trade
Deficits with Some Developing
Nations, 1966

| Country | Soviet Imports | Soviet Exports | Deficit |
|---|---|---|---|
| | | *(million rubles)* | |
| Cuba | 257 | 432 | 175 |
| Yugoslavia | 174 | 193 | 19 |
| Algeria | 5 | 17 | 12 |
| Egypt | 135 | 179 | 44 |
| Iran | 18 | 28 | 10 |
| Iraq | 3 | 32 | 29 |
| Yemen | 1 | 11 | 10 |
| Afghanistan | 17 | 66 | 49 |
| Mongolia | 56 | 142 | 86 |
| North Vietnam | 23 | 61 | 38 |

[7] *Financial Times*, May 12, 1967.
[8] *United Nations Monthly Bulletin of Statistics*, June 1967, pp. xvi-xvii.

## The Conduct of Soviet Foreign Economic Relations

The monopoly nature of Soviet foreign trade, centered in the Ministry of Foreign Trade, was mentioned earlier. The subordinate organizations of the ministry control the entire export and/ or import of various commodities; they also monopolize the provision of services involving economic relations abroad. Thus the foreign tourist in the Soviet Union finds himself completely in the hands of *Intourist*, while anyone outside the Soviet Union wishing to buy that country's books, magazines, or newspapers, or to sell foreign publications to that country, must deal directly or indirectly with *Mezhdunarodnaya Kniga*. In most countries with which the Soviet Union does much business, it maintains trade missions on whose staffs are representatives of the different foreign trade enterprises. In the United States, the function of such a trade mission is performed by a nominally private corporation, Amtorg Trading Corporation, all of whose stock is owned by agencies of the Soviet government.

In theory, such centralization should promote efficiency and economic advantage. Soviet monopoly sellers can pick the most profitable markets while Soviet monopoly buyers can satisfy the country's needs by buying where the best world values are available. No doubt some of these theoretical advantages have been realized, but practice has also shown that there are disadvantages to the system. Many problems arise from the fact that the foreign trade organizations stand between the foreign buyer (or seller) and the Soviet seller (or buyer). Complaints about the results of this situation cover a wide ground. Soviet producers complain they are not informed fully about the demands of foreign buyers and about the climatic and other conditions under which their goods will have to function abroad. Soviet purchasers of foreign goods have sometimes argued that the foreign trade organization did not understand their needs properly and bought the wrong equipment or bought the foreign machinery long before it was actually required (or, sometimes, long after it was first needed). One result of these and similar complaints is that efforts are being made to enable foreign and Soviet buyers and sellers to make direct contact. The Soviet government now encourages foreign firms wishing to sell to Soviet enterprises to advertise in Soviet technical magazines and other Soviet communications media.

At the May 1968 Soviet national economic conference, one economist, Dr. Aleksandrov, proposed that the branch production associations be permitted to engage in foreign trade directly, thus breaking the Ministry of Foreign Trade's monopoly. In reply, the head of *Gosplan*, N. K. Baibakov, rejected the proposal. He argued that the foreign trade monopoly prevents competition between Soviet representatives in foreign markets and keeps to a minimum the cost of conducting foreign trade. Mr. Baibakov did concede it would be advisable to have representatives of producing organizations participate in foreign trade negotiations, presumably as consultants to the Ministry of Foreign Trade's agents.

The historic emphasis on centralized production planning in the Soviet Union has tended to make the Soviet foreign trade system a victim of rigidity, rather than a flexible commercial mechanism able to take quick advantage of opportunities as they arise. One indication of this has been the past Soviet emphasis on bilateral trade agreements. Such an agreement stipulates what and how much the Soviet Union will buy from and sell to another country in a given period—a year or longer. The provisions of such an agreement can then easily be taken into account in drawing up annual and longer term economic plans. The Soviet Union's preference for such bilateral, balanced trade agreements has also been linked to its chronic shortages of foreign exchange. But in order to draw up such balanced trade agreements, the Soviet Union has sometimes had to agree to take goods of lesser importance from its customers or the latter have had to take Soviet goods they really did not want or need. At times, these rigidities have also prevented the Soviet Union from taking advantage of sudden sharp price changes and other shifts in world markets.

Historically, these practices and rigidities developed during the Soviet regime's first decades. In this period Soviet leaders were acutely aware of their economic weaknesses, and so their attitude in the world economy tended to be defensive. They wanted strict control over imports, for example, because they knew their own industries were inefficient and could not compete successfully in price and quality with many foreign goods. Moreover, Stalin was determined to make the Soviet Union self-sufficient, fearing that the country's existence might be threatened if it were dependent upon foreign sources for essential commodities that would be cut off in time of war. In the atmosphere generated by such thinking, economic considerations took second place to political and military goals. The fact that a given commodity could be purchased abroad more cheaply than it could be produced at home played little role in the setting of policy.

Since the mid-1950's, economic considerations have begun to

play an increasingly greater role in Soviet foreign trade planning. Soviet officials now recognize the virtues of the international division of labor, along with the merits of national specialization. Even before the economic reform of late 1965, Soviet leaders and economists had begun to pay much more attention than earlier to trying to calculate the profits and losses of different types of foreign trade in order to obtain bases for rational decision making. The economic reform, with its emphasis on making production profitable, encourages this trend since factories and other Soviet enterprises wish to make profits not only on their domestic sales but also on the business they do with foreign countries.

Complicating the effort to put Soviet foreign trade on a more economic basis have been the deficiencies of Soviet prices, most notably two deficiencies. First, Soviet prices, both before and after the price reform of July 1, 1967, have not adequately reflected relative scarcities in the Soviet Union. Second, the Soviet price system, divorced for decades from world market price trends, bears only slight resemblance to the pattern of world prices. Before 1961, a third factor had further complicated Soviet use of prices as a basis for foreign trade decisions: the notorious overvaluation of the ruble in terms of foreign currencies. In the 1950's, for example, the nominal value of the ruble was declared to be 25 cents. This figure was so out of line with reality that American tourists visiting Moscow were permitted to exchange their dollars at the more realistic rate of one ruble equal to ten cents. The introduction of the heavy ruble on January 1, 1961, was a devaluation that produced a new ruble (equal to ten old rubles) officially valued at $1.11. This new rate more nearly approximated the Soviet currency's true purchasing power parity, in the consumer goods field at least.

Ironically, it was the Eastern European Communist states that first felt the pressures arising in the 1960's from the new Soviet interest in rational foreign trade decision making. Officially, prices in Soviet trade with these countries have been based upon world prices of some period, with adjustments made for special factors. In reality, the provision for adjustments left much room for negotiations in which Soviet bargaining power has not been without influence. Aware of this disparity of bargaining power, many Eastern Europeans have been resentful at what they regarded as Soviet exploitation. They have believed the Soviet Union charged relatively high prices for its products while paying low prices for what it bought.

It came as something of a shock, therefore, in the mid-1960's when Soviet officials and writers began arguing that the Eastern European states were exploiting the Soviet Union. Two factors played a role in prompting these complaints. First, Soviet economists finally realized that Soviet costs of producing raw materials were substantially higher in many cases than world prices. This realization apparently came in the process of revising Soviet prices to take account of interest on capital, rents, and the like. Second, changes in the world price levels used as the bases for Communist nations' trade after 1965 tended to reduce the prices of raw materials sold by the Soviet Union and to increase prices of machinery and other manufactured products the Soviet Union bought from Eastern Europe. As a result of these two developments, Soviet writers began publicly demanding that other Communist states either pay higher prices for Soviet raw materials or contribute substantially to the capital investment needed to expand Soviet output of these raw materials. At times, these demands were accompanied by complaints that the Soviet Union was being cheated because it had to pay world prices for Eastern European machines which did not come up to world quality standards. The Soviet Union hinted that it might choose to stop these purchases and produce for itself the machinery it was buying from Eastern Europe, simultaneously cutting its raw material deliveries to that area.[9] At least one Soviet writer argued in 1966, however, that it would be wrong to raise the prices in the trade of Socialist countries above the world level in order to compensate for the fact that their costs of production are often above world average costs. He urged instead that efforts be concentrated on trying to cut these countries' domestic prices and costs to world levels by improving the technology and organization employed in producing the commodities involved. Quite another line was taken in September 1967 by a writer in the organ of the Ministry of Foreign Trade, A. Alekseyev. He argued that the existing exchange rates of the socialist countries' currencies "create an untrue representation of the effectiveness of trade in particular commodities." He urged changes in these exchange rates to improve the situation.[10]

The stagnation—decline even—of Soviet trade with some Eastern European countries during 1964-1966 may have reflected

---

[9] Cf. for example the article by V. Ladygin and Y. Shirayev in *Voprosy Ekonomiki*, No. 5, 1966, and the article by O. Bogomolov in *Mirovaya Ekonomika i Mezhdunarodniye Otnosheniye*, May 1966.

[10] K. Popov in *Ekonomicheskaya Gazeta*, No. 42, 1966, p. 41, and A. Alekseyev in *Vneshnyaya Torgovlya*, No. 9, 1967, p. 25.

the impact of these new Soviet trade attitudes, as well as of new attitudes in the Eastern European countries which have also been adopting profit-oriented economic reforms. Clearly, both sides are taking a new look at practices that only a few years ago seemed frozen. Ironically, the Soviet complaints about world prices being unfair because they are below Soviet production costs are very similar to the complaints Yugoslav leaders made in 1948 when they broke with the Soviet Union and charged "Soviet exploitation of Yugoslavia." The data on the value of Soviet trade in 1966 and 1967 with its Eastern European allies are not strictly comparable with the similar data for the immediately preceding years. In 1966 a new, modernized set of prices was adopted for trade among Comecon members, one based on average world prices during 1960-1964—a period of declining raw material prices. If prices had not been changed, the 1966 Soviet-Eastern European trade data would have reflected more fully the increase in the physical volume of trade that year.

## The Soviet Union and Comecon

The international economic organization in which the Soviet Union is most active is the Council for Mutual Economic Assistance, or Comecon. Founded in 1949 as an answer to the United States Marshall Plan, Comecon has gone through several phases, ranging from the near inactivity of its early years to the unsuccessful attempt by Khrushchev in 1962 to make it a supranational economic planning body integrating completely the economies of its member states.[11] As of early 1968, Comecon's members were the Soviet Union, East Germany, Hungary, Czechoslovakia, Rumania, Bulgaria, Poland, and Mongolia. Yugoslavia has an official observer status, granted in September 1964. This permits Yugoslav representatives to participate in the work of several key Comecon subgroups. In 1967, Yugoslavia appeared to have stepped up sharply its participation in Comecon activities. Other Communist-ruled nations have from time to time sent observers to meetings of Comecon groups. Albania was a Comecon member in the 1950's, but has not participated since the early 1960's. Given the intense political differences that now divide Communist-ruled states—notably China and the Soviet Union—it seems

---

[11] A brief history of Comecon is given in Schwartz, *The Soviet Economy Since Stalin*, pp. 218-31. For a fuller account, cf. Michael Kaser, *Comecon* (New York: Oxford University Press, Inc., 1965), pp. 9-10.

unlikely Comecon will become, in the foreseeable future, an organization embracing all Communist-ruled states. The peaceful political revolution in Czechoslovakia during early 1968 raised questions about its future participation in Soviet Bloc organizations—including Comecon.

In the non-Communist world, international economic integration is largely guided by market forces. Countries tend to specialize in the production of goods in which they enjoy a comparative advantage, exporting those commodities in which their production costs are relatively low and importing commodities that other nations can produce more cheaply. Similarly, international flows of capital and labor also reflect the search for economic advantage. One example is the diversity of American investments in many foreign countries where high returns are anticipated. Another example is the so-called "brain drain" that has brought many foreign scientists and engineers to the United States where these migrants receive higher salaries than are available in their native lands. The international circulation of goods, capital, and labor is of course far from entirely free in the non-Communist world. It is restricted by tariffs, import quotas, controls over export and import of capital, emigration and immigration laws, and various other measures. Nevertheless, despite these limitations, there exists a closely knit non-Communist world economy characterized by a huge volume of exchanges of goods, services, capital, and labor.

In the Communist nations, the dominance of national economic planning has prevented any such broad, spontaneous integration, and a substitute for the market mechanism has had to be found. Comecon is essentially that substitute, albeit a partial and imperfect substitute. Even with Comecon there is little significant flow of labor across its members' borders and only a very modest trickle of capital investment passes those frontiers. To recognize these deficiencies is not to deny that Comecon has had and still has successes. Under its aegis, the member states have been able to exchange a large amount of technical information and to eliminate substantial amounts of potential duplication in research and development. There are increasing signs, however, that in the future such exchanges of technological data will no longer be free, and that the Soviet Union, the research leader in Comecon, will expect to be paid at world market rates for any technology or patents it hands over to other member states. Similarly, Comecon has facilitated a substantial amount of product specialization among its member states, ending or reducing many kinds of uneconomic duplication of production and facilitating greater division of labor. The unified "Peace" electric power grid uniting the electricity generating systems of Eastern Europe and the European Soviet Union is a major Comecon accomplishment, as is the "Friendship" international pipe line network that now brings Soviet oil from the Volga-Urals area to most of the Eastern European states. Yet these and other Comecon arrangements have on balance produced far less economic integration than has the European Common Market among its member states with their predominantly private enterprise economies.

The difficulties Comecon has encountered in trying to get a more rational division of labor among its member states have been numerous. Some have been technical. Each Comecon member, including the Soviet Union, has an independent and essentially arbitrary and irrational price system; this enormously complicates efforts to make comparisons of costs and returns among member states. Much work has been done in the 1960's in an attempt to improve and unify the national price systems so as to facilitate economic comparisons among member states.

Comecon's deeper problems have political roots. When the organization was originally set up, it consisted of the Soviet Union and a series of puppet states. In this situation it was useful window dressing to provide that decisions could be made only by unanimous vote of all members; in practice the founders were sure that no Comecon member would dare go against Soviet wishes. As time went on, however, Soviet power over the other members weakened and the latter began to defend what they perceived as their national interests. Inevitably, basic conflicts emerged between the more industrialized and less indsutrialized members. The former, notably Czechoslovakia and East Germany, urged that decisions on integration and specialization be taken on the basis of efficiency and cost. But to countries with less industry, such as Rumania and Bulgaria, this approach appeared to lay the groundwork for relegating the less developed member states permanently to the role of suppliers of raw materials and foodstuffs. Hence, the latter urged that considerations of cost and efficiency play a secondary role until all Comecon members had achieved equal levels of industrialization. Nikita Khrushchev sought to break the Gordian knot by proposing a single Comecon planning system that would administer the economies of all members as though they comprised a single nation. The Rumanians thought such a plan would hold back their industrialization and also weaken their national sovereignty. So Bucharest used its veto power to prevent agreement on such comprehensive planning and integration. The result has been that since the early 1960's the Soviet Union has increasingly favored bilateral cooperation with each of Comecon's members individually. This growing emphasis upon bilateral agreements is implicit admission that the high hopes once held for multilateral action through Comecon have been disappointed.

An alternative method of trying to bypass the veto principle in Comecon has been the formation of organizations specifically set up to operate without the veto in specific areas. The leading example is Intermetall which began operation in January 1955 with a membership consisting of East Germany, Poland, Hungary, Bulgaria, Czechoslovakia, and the USSR. Rumania, which insists upon the veto in all matters possibly affecting its national decisions, is not a member of Intermetall. Ultimately, this organization—presumably using computers—will program and direct all the rolling mills of its members so as to supply these nations' needs most economically, regardless of national boundaries. It looks forward also to building large new rolling mills financed by capital investments of all members. In its first years of operation, however, the evidence suggests that much of Intermetall's activity has consisted merely of arranging quarterly meetings at which the members swap excess types and forms of rolled metal.[12]

Still another effort to provide greater flexibility in the mutual economic relations among Comecon members is represented by the International Bank for Economic Cooperation (IBEC) whose members are the nations belonging to Comecon. Operating since the beginning of 1964, the IBEC seeks primarily to provide a system of multilateral clearings among its members to replace the largely bilateral character of their earlier trade. Theoretically, each Comecon member can seek balance through the bank by offsetting its trade surpluses with some members against its trade deficits with others. For this purpose, the IBEC keeps tabs on the mutual trade of its members in terms of a common bookkeeping unit, the so-called transferable ruble, equal in nominal value to the ordinary ruble. The IBEC also helps to finance trade among its members by extending credits to cover tempo-

---

[12] A. Zubkov, "Segodnyashny Den 'Intermetalla'," *Mezhdunarodnaya Zhizn,* No. 7, 1967, pp. 146-47.

rary deficits arising from seasonal or other forces. A country that has an overall trade surplus with all its fellow Comecon members has the amount of that surplus in transferable rubles, credited in its IBEC account. Unfortunately, this surplus is normally not usable for purchases in nations outside Comecon. This restriction led to pressure from Poland to give the IBEC resources in gold and convertible currencies (that is, in American dollars, French francs, and the like) so that countries with an overall surplus in Comecon trade might eventually get resources to use in the non-Communist world. The decision to take a first step toward this goal was finally made in April 1966. Later that year, the IBEC members contributed the equivalent of 30 million transferable rubles (about $33 million) in gold and convertible currencies to the Bank's capital. As of the end of 1966, the IBEC had a total paid-in capital of 89.7 million transferable rubles, of which about 40 per cent had been contributed by the Soviet Union, about 18 per cent by East Germany, and smaller amounts by other members. With these resources, the IBEC was expanding its operations in world money markets and beginning to make arrangements to help finance the trade of non-Comecon members—presumably, mainly underdeveloped countries—with all Comecon nations through the use of accounts in transferable rubles. In 1966 the IBEC's total turnover was 36.7 billion transferable rubles, as against 35.9 billion in 1965 and 32.5 billion in 1964. [13]

At the time of this writing, the IBEC is still a young institution. In time it may conceivably be of major importance in helping to create genuinely multilateral trade among Comecon members. So far the general impression Western bankers and other observers have gained is that the Bank has failed as yet to provide a major breakthrough in the effort to shift from bilateralism to multilateralism. The situation may change drastically some day when and if member nations' balances in transferable rubles can be exchanged fully for gold or hard currency. But despite the small beginnings made toward giving the bank resources of gold and convertible currency, the time of full convertibility of the transferable ruble still seems distant.

The international financial prospects of both the Soviet Union and the IBEC would be radically improved, of course, if the United States and other Western countries were to devalue their

---

[13] The 1966 annual report of the IBEC is summarized at length in *Ekonomicheskaya Gazeta*, No. 25, June 1967, pp. 42-43.

currencies by increasing the price of gold. As the world's second largest gold producer, the Soviet Union would be one of the prime beneficiaries of such a change. Soviet spokesmen vigorously urged such an increase in the world gold price in late 1967 when Britain devalued the pound sterling and in early 1968 when the American dollar came under attack.

As Comecon approaches its twentieth birthday, the organization's complex structure reflects the many areas of its work. Heading its organizational chart is the Council Session of the Council for Mutual Economic Assistance, attended by the Communist party chiefs and by the premiers of member states. The Council has met infrequently, however, and the chief responsibility for overseeing the functioning of Comecon is normally borne by the Executive Committee. This body consists of one deputy premier from each member state. It meets several times a year. The day-to-day work of Comecon is supervised by the Secretariat which has its headquarters in Moscow and which has always been headed by a Soviet citizen. The detailed work of Comecon is done in permanent technical commissions covering most major economic fields. These working groups exist for chemicals, ferrous metals, oil and gas, light industry, geology, peaceful uses of atomic energy, and machinery production, among others. There are also general departments which deal with such subjects as coordination of statistics, foreign trade, currency and finance, standardization, the exchange of economic and technical information, and the like. Each of the major commissions and departments may establish subgroups to handle particular detailed matters. Normally, representatives of all member states participate in the work of these specialized organs.[14]

The most general task performed in Comecon is the attempted coordination of the five year plans of member states. It is symptomatic of Rumania's success in changing the orientation of Comecon that the announcement of the beginning of coordination work for plans covering 1971-1975 stressed that this would include bilateral consultations as well as multilateral negotiations. The Comecon Executive Committee Communique reporting on the meeting of July 5-7, 1967, stated the nature of this coordinating activity in the following terms:

> The coordination of plans must cover in the first case the basic branches of industry and of transportation serving the interna-

[14] An organizational chart of Comecon is given in the end papers of Kaser, *Comecon.*

tional exchange of goods. It must also take into account the perspectives for the development of science and technology.

The content of the work for coordinating plans on a bilateral basis will be agreed upon directly between the interested countries, starting out from the necessity of the all-sided examination of the problems of mutual interest advanced by the countries concerned. Individual economic problems of cooperation in whose solution the members belonging to the Council have expressed interest will be examined and worked on in complete fashion on a multilateral basis.

It is intended that the examinations will relate to problems of international production specialization and cooperation, of standardization, of the coordination among the interested countries of the construction of individual projects, of cooperation in the carrying out of geological explorations and of questions making possible the development of mutual trade.

The Executive Committee has recommended to countries belonging to Comecon that they carry out negotiations and conclude in the 2nd and 3rd quarters of 1970 bilateral long term agreements about mutual deliveries of goods among Comecon member countries during 1971-1975. In addition they should conclude, so far as they are ready to do so, other economic cooperation agreements taking into account the results of work carried out on the coordination of national economic plans.[15]

The implication of this statement would seem to be that in the future the burden of such coordination will fall more on bilateral consultations than upon multilateral consultations involving all members of Comecon.

If we look briefly to the future of Soviet foreign economic relations, two forecasts, at least, seem justified. For one, most probably the volume of Soviet foreign trade will increase, particularly with the non-Communist world. In this connection there seems every likelihood that once the war in Vietnam ends, the United States will lift or ease many of the legal and other barriers which have kept Soviet-American commerce small since the late 1940's. Second, the role of non-commodity exchanges will grow sharply in Soviet economic relations with the outside world. Already during the past decade Western tourism in the Soviet Union has grown greatly, but there is vast room for further expansion. Soviet government interest in this area is indicated by such moves as the decision to build more hotels and the decision to restore and refurbish the ancient Central European Russian

---

[15] *Ekonomicheskaya Gazeta*, No. 28, July 1967, p. 42.

monastery town of Suzdal, making it a tourist and a convention center of world importance on the model of, say, Colonial Williamsburg in the United States. Similarly the mid-1965 action of the Soviet Union in becoming a party to the Paris Convention providing for international protection of patent rights was a historic change of policy. The Soviet Union has become a major purchaser of foreign licenses and technical know-how as a means of speeding up its own advance. It is also very interested in becoming a major seller of patents, licenses, and know-how to other countries, and has already had some significant successes. This is all a very far cry from the years in which Russians regarded patent protection as a capitalist imposition and stole Western technology with an easy conscience as often as they could. But in those earlier days, of course, the Soviet Union had little or nothing to patent and to sell to others. One must have property, after all, before the virtues of protecting property rights become completely convincing.

The opening of direct New York-Moscow commercial air service on July 15, 1968 gave a particularly vivid sign of the growth of Soviet economic connections with the West. More than a decade of involved and often-interrupted negotiations had been required before the first regularly scheduled Aeroflot and Pan-American jets landed in New York and Moscow to begin this direct link between the world's two most powerful nations.

# The Future of the Soviet Economy

**8**

In past decades it was fashionable to refer to the "Soviet experiment." The passage of time has made the phrase obsolete. Now that the Soviet society and economy have passed the half century mark, both friend and foe agree that a viable and mature nation has replaced Czarist Russia. Analysts trying to envisage this society's future can now project from more than five decades of experience. And, except perhaps for Chinese and other followers of Mao Tse-tung, these analysts tend to look for evolution, not revolution, in the economic and other institutions of the Soviet Union. A thermonuclear war would change all present forecasts of the Soviet future as well as of the future of the world. Here, however, we shall assume that no such catastrophe will occur, and also that the Soviet Union will continue in the years ahead—as it has ever since 1945—to avoid participation in any major conflict.

It is probably useful at this point to remember how often the prophets, Soviet and foreign alike, have been wrong about that country's economic prospects. In the late 1950's Nikita Khrushchev exulted in his nation's rapid advance. By 1970, he predicted, the Soviet Union would have caught up with and gone beyond the United States. By 1980, he assured his people, the Soviet Union would be on the threshold of Communism. He gave world-wide publicity to his detailed estimates of the enormous increases Soviet production would achieve by 1980. Following Khrushchev's involuntary exit from office in 1964, his successors have shown more modesty. Tacitly, and sometimes even explicitly, his forecasts have been recognized as "harebrained" and relegated into deserved oblivion. In the early and mid-1960's, some Western observers tended to commit the opposite error. Seeing the stagnation of agriculture in many of these years and the accompanying tendency of the rate of growth of Soviet industrial output to slow down, they began to dismiss the idea of any serious Soviet economic challenge to the United States. But as this is written there are signs of second thoughts in the West. In 1966 and 1967, Soviet industry and agriculture staged a remarkable comeback from the worst levels of the Khrushchev slump a few years earlier. And despite the production stimulus provided by the Vietnam War, the United States suffered high level economic stagnation for a time during 1966-1967.

Yet despite the prophets' past errors of optimism and pessimism, one fact is indisputable. The Soviet economy is a growth mechanism with tremendous built-in momentum. The amount of that growth can vary from year to year in response to many factors, but every year since 1946 Soviet national income has been higher than it was the year before. There is no reason to suppose that this will change in the foreseeable period ahead. The regime's basic commitment to economic development has survived all past changes of leadership as has the policy of a high rate of investment—the motor behind this production ascent. In the mid-1960's, the Soviet gross national product was roughly $350 billion annually. It is by no means unreasonable to suppose that, in the same prices, it will reach or exceed $400 billion by 1970, and $600 billion by 1980. These are not extravagant estimates in the light of the record since they merely assume, for example, that the average annual rate of Soviet GNP growth in the 1970's will be 4 per cent. A less likely case can be made that by 1980 Soviet GNP may be in the $700-750 billion range. If that higher level were attained, total Soviet production in 1980 would be at about the level of the United States in 1965 and 1966. It would have to be divided, however, among a population of 260-300,000,000 people, 30-50 per cent more than the American population in the mid-1960's. Put another way, barring a major depression in the United States in the next decade and a half or so, there seems no danger that the Soviet Union will overtake the United States economically by 1980. On the other hand, a return to the pattern of slow and interrupted economic growth that characterized the American economy in the 1950's could see the huge United States lead whittled down significantly.

A detailed analysis to justify the forecast made above would require more space than is available here, but a few key factors can be pointed out.

On the positive side, there is every reason to suppose that major productivity improvements are ahead in the Soviet Union. There is still much advanced Western technology that is only little utilized in the Soviet Union, but which that country clearly intends to tap, even at the cost of buying the needed know-how and machinery from the West. The increasingly educated and skilled Soviet labor force is a rich asset that should produce more abundant dividends in the years ahead. Soviet agricultural performance in 1966 and 1967 indicated that substantially improved farm production can be obtained. The key is to provide those who work the land better price and wage incentives, more adequate supplies of machinery, fertilizer, and insecticides, and the resources for larger investments in irrigation and land drainage projects. Finally, additional impetus for economic growth is provided by the new Soviet emphasis on rational economic calculation. This is evident in the economic reform of September 1965 and in the attempt to improve economic planning through the increased use of modern econometric methods.

There are, of course, forces which will tend to retard growth. Increasingly, the Soviet Union is becoming dependent upon oil, gas, and other natural resources obtained in Siberian areas where huge investments will be required to provide houses, schools, roads, and other basic infrastructure as well as to build productive facilities. A good deal of capital has already been assigned to the major program for extraordinarily rapid economic development of the Soviet Far East between 1967 and 1975. That program, announced in July 1967, has clearly been framed with an eye to possible future danger from China rather than on the basis of purely economic considerations. The threat of increasing Chinese missile and nuclear weapon strength has apparently already induced the Soviet leadership to begin investing in a major national anti-missile system that could cost many billions of rubles. Increased military drains could arise also from intensified Soviet-American hostility. Finally, in the decade of the 1970's there may be manpower problems arising from the fact that the supply of new entrants into the labor force will decline, reflecting the sharp reduction in births during the first half of the 1960's.

On balance, however, the likelihood is that the Soviet Union, already richer than ever before in its history, will become far richer in the decades that lie ahead. Some of this wealth will undoubtedly go to bolstering both the sinews and the symbols of Soviet power. By 1980 there may well be a manned Soviet base on the moon and several large permanent Soviet stations in space. The Soviet armed forces will have been re-equipped with even more advanced weapons than they have now. But inevitably part of this new wealth will go to the Soviet people whose craving for more and better housing, goods, and services is still very far from satisfied despite the substantial gains since World War II. In the past decade the Soviet people were exposed to the first flood of television sets, transistor radios, refrigerators, washing machines, and even electric shavers. By the 1970's these and other fruits of "gadget Communism" should become commonplace household possessions. Then the new status symbol—owned by five million or more Soviet citizens by 1980—will be the automobile. Soviet entry into the age of widespread car ownership will require large investments in the hitherto relatively neglected road network, as well as in gasoline and repair stations, highway motels and restaurants, radar equipment to detect speeders, and special institutes to study the problem of combating air pollution from automobile exhausts. By past Soviet standards, though not by American standards, the Soviet Union will probably become an affluent society by 1980. The gulf between Russia and the poverty stricken underdeveloped nations, including China, is already wide; it promises to become far wider.

With the growth of the consumer economy of the Soviet Union, there is likely to be increased buyer sophistication, taste, and fashion consciousness with the attendant problems for producers. The international fashion show held in Moscow in September 1967 is undoubtedly a harbinger of things to come. The goods famine that plagued the country during the 1930's, 1940's, and much of the 1950's is gone with respect to many ordinary commodities; now consumers can often afford to wait until they get the style, the cut, or the color they want. Very poor quality goods increasingly find no market regardless of price. It is the realization of these complications that has spurred the recent interest among Soviet executives in market research, advertising, and close, direct relations between consumer goods factories and the stores selling their products. The art of salesmanship, so long derided and neglected, is likely to assume an increasing importance as the members of a richer Soviet society face a wider range of choices and have an ever greater opportunity to exercise the capriciousness with which Western consumers plague Western merchants.

Service industries, so long and so notoriously starved in the Soviet Union, will assume ever greater importance. Already millions of Soviet television set owners know the frustrations of trying to get that device fixed because of shortages of both repairmen and spare parts. Ahead lies the nightmare of trying to provide facilities and personnel for the repair of Soviet automobiles as they multiply. But even before then the Soviet Union needs many thousands of additional dry cleaning shops, laundries, tailors, beauty parlors, plumbing and electrical repair contractors, and, eventually perhaps, even computer dating services. On September 13, 1967, *Pravda* published a decree ordering major expansion of the facilities and personnel needed to improve Soviet services.

The evolution of Soviet economic institutions will continue; certain fundamentals, though, particularly the state ownership and operation of most industries, capital, and the like, will remain. The dogmatic opposition to small scale private trade and private artisan activity may well weaken as a more confident Soviet Union appreciates the value of and feels less threatened by the small cobbler shop employing a few hired workers and the petty merchant buying flowers or vegetables or fruits from farmers for resale in the city. It is not unreasonable to suppose that a partial step in this direction was taken by a government decision announced in *Izvestiya*, September 26, 1967. This authorized collective farms, state farms, and organizations set up by several *kolkhozy* acting jointly to form ancillary workshops to produce consumer goods and processed foods that could be sold directly to the population. But there is no return to capitalism—in the sense of private ownership of large parts of the nation's productive capital—in sight.

This latter conclusion does not, of course, deny the possibility that many of the trends initiated in the economic reform of September 1965 will be further developed. Powerful forces are exerting pressure for even greater freedom for enterprises than the limited measure granted by the reform. Professor Liberman and others have already written publicly about the virtues of competition among enterprises and have urged that some categories of prices be permitted to fluctuate in response to supply and demand rather than being set rigidly from the center. Professor Kantorovich and other mathematical economists have rebuffed those who thought they saw in linear programming, input-output analysis, and the use of computers a new means of reintroducing detailed central planning of the entire economy. An important degree of central planning is virtually certain to persist for the indefinite future, however, just as there is now substantial central economic planning in the United States, most of Western Europe, and Japan. But the chances seem good that the area covered by central planning in the Soviet Union will diminish with time as heads of enterprises and other executives learn to exercise more initiative and to utilize the new opportunities opened up by the changes already made. One may speculate that eventually the Soviet Union may have a socialist market economy roughly similar to the Yugoslav model, with the market providing much of the economic coordination now provided by the central planners in Moscow. But that development, if it ever comes, is not likely to be realized in the presently foreseeable future.

It would be in the spirit of recent Soviet economic trends for the monetary and banking system to assume a much more active role in economic life. There is already discussion of making credit available to those enterprises that are prepared to pay the best price, that is, offer the highest rate of interest. One force which may further this trend is the accumulation of free balances in the special funds set up for enterprises by the 1965 economic reform. It may be that each of ten factories does not have enough capital in its fund for the expansion of production to do very much for itself. But it has already occurred to some Soviet bankers that in such a case a factory might be better off lending its idle balance to another enterprise willing to pay a satisfactory rate of interest. Such possibilities may be visionary in the late 1960's. They could be realities in the 1970's.

Major changes may be ahead, too, in the field of consumer credit, though the day of the Soviet credit card is probably not just around the corner. The existing Soviet consumer credit system covers a relatively narrow spectrum of goods and requires a relatively quick pay-back period by Western standards. Nevertheless it has grown rapidly, increasing more than five-fold between 1960 and 1965. In 1965, the volume of this consumer credit exceeded $3.5 billion, with clothing sales and consumer durable goods sales on credit each exceeding $1 billion that year.[1] Future growth in this area seems very likely.

Important institutional changes have been taking place in agriculture, and there are signs more will come soon. The differences between the collective farms and the state farms have been dramatically narrowed in the years since Stalin's death, and the possibility of their eventual amalgamation into one system grows more probable. Now collective farmers are theoretically guaranteed the same wages as state farm workers, the collective and state farms both own their machinery, and those state farms transferred to full *khozraschet* receive the same prices for their produce as do the *kolkhozy*. Further radical changes are in the air. Some Soviet economists urge that farms be allowed to plan their own activities guided only by the relative prices and costs of different crops and livestock rather than by directives or contracts covering what they must produce or what they must sell to the state. Experiments carried out in recent years have studied the practicability of leasing substantial tracts of land to small groups of workers equipped with all the machinery needed to work an area perhaps comparable to a substantial Iowa farm. Here, as in many other areas of Soviet life, the patterns originally evolved in the late 1920's and the 1930's are being scrutinized critically by new and less dogmatic minds.

The Soviet Union, in short, is very much an economy in transition. It has left the grinding poverty of the past and can begin to glimpse the possibilities of comfort and welfare on a level now familiar in Western Europe. It is deviating further from Stalin's brutal and wasteful command economy and moving toward a more subtly articulated economic mechanism that may be capable of meeting the varied wishes of consumers as well as the priority military and other needs of the state. The fruits of decades of sacrifice and deprivation are finally beginning to be harvested.

Yet some cautionary notes are in order, too. There are, for example, no sure guarantees against retrogression. The implementation of the economic reform in industry and elsewhere since September 1965 has met the silent, but determined and often ef-

---

[1] *Narkhoz 1965*, p. 634.

fective, sabotage and opposition of those who fear that their own power and position are threatened by the present trends. A worsening of the international situation or some new convulsion in the Kremlin ruling body could put more dogmatic men at the helm, leaders who might try to undo the changes already made. Also, problems are likely to arise from another direction. Human wants are insatiable, and sometimes appetites grow faster than their satisfaction. In the wake of the Negro riots in some American cities in the late 1960's, it was frequently pointed out that these disturbances had come after a period of rapid gains, but that Negro aspirations had risen more rapidly. The possibility of difficulties arising from a similar Soviet phenomenon cannot be dismissed, especially in an era when television, radio, and travel opportunities have made millions of Soviet citizens more aware of the gap between their own situation and that of workers and farmers in Western industrialized nations. The pressure of Soviet young people for greater freedom could have important economic consequences in the future.

At this writing, the cold war begun shortly after World War II has existed for a generation, yet vast changes have taken place on both sides of the ideological barrier. Neither the United States nor the Soviet Union is the same nation it was when Winston Churchill gave his historic warning at Fulton, Missouri, and when Stalin was fastening his grip upon a helpless Eastern Europe. In the late 1960's the actual differences in the manner in which economic life is directed and governed in the United States and the Soviet Union are narrower than ever. The United States has learned the importance of government-promoted rapid economic growth, while the Soviet Union has learned the importance of a more rational and more consumer-oriented economy. Major differences remain, and presumably they will persist indefinitely. Yet these differences are minor as compared to the common interest of both the Soviet and American people in avoiding thermonuclear destruction. The overriding issue was well stated by President John F. Kennedy when he declared at American University on June 10, 1963:

> Today, should total war ever break out again—no matter how —our two countries will be the primary targets. It is an ironic but accurate fact that the two strongest powers are the two in the most danger of devastation. All we have built, all we have worked for, would be destroyed in the first 24 hours. And even in the cold war . . . our two countries bear the heaviest burdens.

For we are both devoting to weapons massive sums of money that could be better devoted to combat ignorance, poverty and disease.

We are both caught up in a vicious and dangerous cycle with suspicion on one side breeding suspicion on the other, and new weapons begetting counter-weapons.

The key question remains how to end that "vicious and dangerous cycle" so that the enormous capabilities of both Soviet and American economies can be turned from massive preoccupation with the weapons of death to concentration on exploiting the enormous possibilities for making all men's lives richer, freer, and longer.

# Index